THIERRY HENRY

FIFTY DEFINING FIXTURES

THIERRY HENRY
FIFTY DEFINING FIXTURES

Paul Joseph

AMBERLEY

For Lydia & Louis

First published 2014

Amberley Publishing
The Hill, Stroud
Gloucestershire, GL5 4EP

www.amberley-books.com

British Library Cataloguing in Publication Data.
A catalogue record for this book is available from the British Library.

ISBN 978 1 4456 4226 0 (print)
ISBN 978 1 4456 4248 2 (ebook)

Typesetting and Origination by Amberley Publishing.
Printed in the UK.

Contents

Introduction

His sensational career was down simply to Thierry's class. He is a player who had everything you dream of as a manager – physical potential, a technical level, super intelligence and what people also forget for many top level athletes is he was dedicated to his job, with a very serious life. He is simply a model professional who won everything you can in our world – Thierry, you were really special.

Arsène Wenger
December 2011

The story of Thierry Daniel Henry, born 17 August 1977, is not quite the archetypal rags-to-riches yarn. Nor is it an allegorical tale of transformation or redemption. Rather more prosaically, Henry's path to greatness was laid out with calculated precision – give or take the odd error of judgement by the man himself and those who professed to be acting in his interests.

Without a great need to weave an emotional narrative through his life and career, we are left with the refreshing task of viewing his achievements in footballing terms alone. In that regard, there is little doubt that Henry will be remembered as one of his generation's most enthralling performers.

That is not to say he was without contradiction on the pitch; despite in many ways being a consummate entertainer, a furrowed brow was never far from his face. Often heard stressing the importance of the team over the individual, on occasion he was an overbearing presence who could inhibit teammates. This paradoxical side to Henry was probably why he never quite achieved universal adoration; an opaque miasma surrounding his character, meaning it was never quite as easy to love Henry the man as it was Henry the footballer.

But what a footballer. For twenty years, Henry has captivated us with his supreme athleticism, astuteness and grace. But what is also noticeable is that his all-encompassing playing style makes him virtually impossible to categorise. Ask a fan about Henry and they can appear almost lost for words, reduced to gushing platitudes that reveal both nothing and everything. It is such dumbstruck reverence that suggests of a man who transcended his sport.

Choosing the Fifty

To whittle down the works of a maestro to fifty pieces would be challenging whatever the craft. With sport, the temptation is to approach the task using quantitative methodology, choosing the games that had measurable outcomes such as trophies, goals or Man of the Match champagne bottles. But to do so would be a dereliction of duty. Henry's career has been defined by so much more than a collection of numbers, and so my efforts required a more delicate touch.

Of course, many of the matches selected themselves, and they take their rightful place in this book. But football fans being as they are, others are ripe for debate.

Thierry Henry has played over 700 professional games and counting. What follows is a wistful look back at fifty whose impact extended beyond the full-time whistle. I like to think he would agree with at least a handful of my choices.

Paul Joseph
August 2014

AS Monaco 6 RC Lens 0
Ligue 1, 28 April 1995

Behind every great footballer there are those who played an instrumental role in their development but are often reduced to mere footnotes in history. In the case of Thierry Henry, there are several such unsung figures.

It is often Arsène Wenger who is credited as the great guiding influence in Henry's early career, but beyond giving him his professional debut as a left-winger for AS Monaco in August 1994, Wenger was only a fleeting presence in that nascent period of his education.

Indeed, youth coaches Claude Chezelles, Thierry Prêt and Jean-Marie Panza, who all harnessed Henry's talents through his adolescent years, can each lay greater claim than Wenger to the mantle of being his first true mentor. So too the scout Arnold Catalano, who plucked a thirteen-year-old Henry from the Paris suburbs and asked him to join Monaco after watching him score six goals in a local youth game.

Henry's initial first-team appearances, coming at the start of Monaco's 1994/95 season, were not the greatest endorsement that he was ready for regular action. But if Wenger had intended to keep faith with Henry during his teething period, those plans were scuppered when he was fired after just seven games of the season, with Monaco languishing three points off the relegation zone. Wenger, who had won the Ligue 1 title and the Coupe de France during his seven-year spell in the principality, would have to wait several years to wield his nurturing powers on Henry's career.

With Wenger gone, former Monaco players Jean Petit and Jean-Luc Ettori were named as caretaker managers and they remained in place until February, when youth academy coach Gerard Banide was put in the hot-seat until the end of the season. Understandably, the temporary bosses chose to play it safe by relying on more experienced squad members and as a consequence Henry found himself sidelined.

In fairness to them, the policy worked and by the time RC Lens came to visit the Stade Louis II in late April, Monaco had recovered their form to the extent that they were now contenders for a place in the top six and potential qualification for the following season's UEFA Cup.

Team: Porato, Dumas, Blondeau, Di Meco, Petersen, Puel, Legwinski (73), Scifo, Petit, Madar (22), Djorkaeff
Subs: Henry (22), Viaud (73)

Arsène Wenger's decision to hand Henry his debut against Nice back in August had been somewhat forced upon him by an injury list that left him bereft of attacking options, with Brazilian striker Sonny Anderson his one striker of repute. A graduate of the elite Clairefontaine academy, the now seventeen-year-old Henry had shown enough promise to convince Wenger that he deserved a chance in the absence of his older, more established counterparts.

Despite failing to make an impact in his early turnouts on the left wing for Monaco, Henry caught the eye in September, scoring a brace for the French Juniors against England. After the game, France's National Technical Director (and later manager of Liverpool), Gérard Houllier, spoke about him in glowing terms:

He has the capacity to beat defenders. He's very good with the ball at his feet. He's also got great potential in terms of power, which he can use to go past opponents. He's a striker for the future. When he has got his finishing right, he'll be very close to the top level.

At this embryonic stage of his career, there was no shame in Henry still needing to improve in front of goal. But what was already clear for all to see was his ingenuity and capacity to find the right solution in a split second and in any situation on the pitch, and it was those very talents that he would display against Lens in a match that, for the first time, brought him to the wider public attention.

Early in the match, Monaco striker Madar suffered a head injury and Henry, sporting short dreadlocks and a thin moustache, trotted on to replace him upfront. He had flattered to deceive in all of his run-outs from the bench so far (the majority of which saw him playing on the wing) and there was no obvious reason to imagine his latest opportunity would be any different. But just 4 minutes after coming on, Henry scored his first goal as a professional footballer – a goal of invention, spontaneity and technique.

It came when a Lens defender played a loose pass that was collected by Monaco striker Djorkaeff 25 yards from goal. Djorkaeff evaded a tackle and slipped the ball through for Henry, who had managed to stay onside.

The pass was a little heavy and it left Henry with a straight chase with the Lens goalkeeper Warmuz (who later played with Henry at Arsenal) to reach it first. Henry was too quick for him but his touch took him away from goal, almost to the edge of the penalty area and at a seemingly impossible angle to score. He steadied himself and curled a pinpoint shot above the heads of the frantically retreating Lens defenders and into the top corner of the net.

Before the first half was out Henry scored a second, this time with a simple pass into an empty net after a shot was parried into his path by Warmuz. Lens went on to win the game 6-0 and Henry had amplified the murmurs of interest around him that would before long grow into a resounding chorus.

AS Monaco 4 Bayer Leverkusen 0
Champions League Group Match
1 October 1997

The two seasons that followed Henry's first goals as a professional against RC Lens had seen his stock rise to the point that by 1997 he was being talked of as a genuine contender for the following year's France World Cup squad.

Not that it had all been plain sailing. Under the stewardship of Monaco coach Jean Tigana, who in the summer of 1995 had been appointed as Arsène Wenger's permanent replacement, Henry continued to be used primarily off of the substitutes' bench. In the 1995/96 season he made just twenty-two appearances, scoring three times, as Tigana relied on the more recognised Anderson, Madar and Ikpeba as the attacking triumvirate in his preferred 4-3-3 formation.

While he was yet to establish himself at club level, he had received great acclaim playing for the French Under-18s. In the summer of 1996, he was part of an all-star squad of Clairefontaine scholars, including William Gallas, Mikaël Silvestre, Nicolas Anelka and David Trezeguet, that secured victory in the UEFA European Under-18s Championship, with Henry scoring the winning goal in the final versus Spain.

Under the tutelage of Under-18s coach Gerard Houllier, who had made Henry captain and also gave him a number of opportunities playing as a striker (only the emergence of Monaco teammate David Trezeguet would see Henry return to the wing), Henry grew in confidence and stature – traits that would soon transfer to his club form.

While Henry was not yet established as a first-choice starter, season 1996/97 was unquestionably his breakthrough campaign, recording ten goals and thirteen assists in forty-eight appearances as Monaco won the Ligue 1 championship. To add to his League title winner's medal, Henry was also named French Young Footballer of the Year and ended the season captaining the French Under-21s to European Championship victory.

There was, however, a sour note to an otherwise distinguished season when he was caught up in an alleged scandal involving a botched attempt by Spanish giants Real Madrid to capture his signature. According to the journalist Philippe Auclair's biography on Henry, Real were erroneously told that the player's Monaco contract would expire a year earlier than was correct, leading to Henry signing a pre-contract agreement with the Spaniards. The saga ended with Henry and the Spanish club both receiving substantial FIFA fines for breaching transfer rules and the player himself returning to Monaco with his tail tucked firmly between his legs. In an effort to protect their young asset from such shenanigans ever taking place again, Monaco coerced a repentant Henry into extending his contract at the club.

In the fall-out to the whole unseemly affair, which by all accounts had a profound effect on Henry as a person, he was virtually frozen out of the Monaco side for nearly three months. He returned as Monaco resumed their UEFA Cup campaign at the quarter-final phase, and it would be Henry's first taste of European success as Monaco went on to reach the semi-finals of the competition. But the following season would see him make a mark on the biggest European club stage of all.

Henry's contribution as Monaco progressed to the semi-finals of the 1997/98 UEFA Champions League was in stark contrast to his role in their domestic campaign, in which he remained an infrequent starter. Yet in Europe it was a different story, with Henry starting seven of Monaco's ten games on their way to the semis, contributing a hugely impressive seven goals.

In none of those matches did Henry make a greater impact than Monaco's home match against German club Bayer Leverkusen in the second round of group fixtures.

Team: Barthez, Pignol, Konjic (46), Dumas, Djetou, Collins, Legwinski (54), Henry, N'Doram (73), Trezeguet, Ikpeba
Subs: Irles (46), Christanval (54), Benarbia (73)

Monaco's Champions League debut had offered scant evidence that they were equipped to progress beyond the group phase, let alone reach the later stages of the competition. A comprehensive 3-0 defeat away to Portuguese side Sporting Lisbon meant that their next game, at home to Bayer Leverkusen, was a must-win.

For Henry, the game was lent added importance by the fact that a few days after the game, France coach Aimé Jacquet was due to name his squad for a friendly against South Africa. With the World Cup just eight months away, Henry was desperate to force himself into Jacquet's plans.

Having missed the defeat in Portugal through suspension, Henry was restored to the starting line-up, playing on the left wing with N'Doram, Trezeguet and Ikpeba selected upfront.

With 30 minutes of the match gone, Henry gave Monaco the lead with the kind of finish that would become his trademark. A throw-in on Monaco's left flank was worked back out to Henry, who was lurking on the edge of the penalty box. As a defender slid in, Henry judged the situation perfectly, knowing his opponent would not reach it, and allowed the ball to roll into his feet. With the defender prostrate, Henry looked up to see a glut of players between him and the goal. Spotting the only route through, he guided a beautiful side-footed shot beyond the goalkeeper's reach and into the far corner.

The score remained the same until the 72nd minute, when Monaco extended their lead, with Henry heavily involved again. A fractionally overhit pass was played over the top into Monaco's inside-left channel, leaving Henry to give chase. With the ball looking likely to run out of play for a goal kick, the Leverkusen goalkeeper rushed off his line and Henry spotted an opportunity. Reaching the ball fractionally before him, Henry acrobatically lifted the ball back into the penalty area where Ikpeba was lurking. He composed himself and lashed a ferocious shot high into the net to put Monaco 2-0 up.

Far from settling on their lead, Monaco continued to attack and with 7 minutes left they made it three thanks to another fine finish by Henry. Some neat midfield trickery released Ikpeba, who surged towards goal. As he entered the penalty area he checked his run but in the process lost control of the ball, only for Henry to step forward and curl an unstoppable shot into the top corner.

On 90 minutes, Henry book-ended his most complete club performance so far by creating a fourth goal for Monaco, putting the tie well and truly to bed in the process. Collecting the ball just inside his own half, Henry turned and played a pass between the Leverkusen defence for Ikpeba to run on to. Finding himself clean through on goal, Ikpeba's first shot was saved but after collecting the rebound he tried again and this time the ball found its way into the net courtesy of a deflection on the line.

In one match, Henry had displayed the full gamut of his talents and he was subsequently selected for the South Africa friendly ten days later. While he struggled to make an impact in that game (and was left out of every French squad for the following six months) Henry's European exploits helped to convince Aimé Jacquet to take him to the World Cup finals to be played on home soil later that summer.

Italy 0 France 0
(France Won on Penalties)
World Cup Quarter-Finals
3 July 1998

The spectre of the 1998 World Cup, which was to be hosted by France for the first time in sixty years, had lingered over Henry for what must have seemed a lifetime. He had experienced a season of mixed fortunes with Monaco, lighting up the Champions League as they reached the semi-finals, but only appearing sporadically and mainly from the substitutes' bench in domestic matches. Having won the French Young Player of the Year award two years earlier, his expected emergence as one of the game's brightest talents had veered slightly off course.

As a consequence, when French coach Aimé Jacquet prepared to name his official World Cup squad in early May, Henry was by no means a shoo-in. Several other young candidates, including Arsenal's Nicolas Anelka, had put up strong cases for their selection and there was only so much room for raw, unproven players on such a high-stakes stage.

After months of speculation, the announcement finally came and Henry had made the cut (Anelka had not). Just four years after making his professional debut, the twenty-year-old was now set to appear at the world's most prestigious sporting festival.

It was not only footballing ambitions that were at stake, but also the chance to be part of a truly epochal moment in the history of a country. The 1990s had been a miserable decade for France, with rising unemployment, industrial unrest and racial violence creating a tense and fractious milieu. For so long the most racially divided country in Europe, the World Cup was hailed as an opportunity to create a genuine sense of national unity through the ethnically diverse make-up of the French squad. As one of several black players in a squad containing men of Algerian, Armenian, Basque, African and Caribbean descent, Henry was a key symbol of what would come to be known as France's 'rainbow team' of 1998.

But France could not allow itself to get distracted by cultural or socio-political navel-gazing, because the only way this tournament would resonate beyond football was if they achieved success on the pitch. For so long the country had failed to live up to its undoubted footballing talents and coach Jacquet had gone to great lengths to instil a discipline and will-to-win that many felt had been lacking in previous competitions.

If Henry had been overjoyed at his inclusion in the squad, he must have thought he was dreaming when he was selected to start France's opening match against South Africa at the Stade Vélodrome in Marseille. Not only did he start (on the right of a three-pronged attack), he also got on the score sheet, notching the third goal in a comprehensive 3-0 victory.

Six days later, Henry went one better, scoring a brace as France beat Saudi Arabia 4-0 at the State de France in Paris, ensuring their progress to the knockout stages of the competition. Even without setting the World Cup alight, Henry had already surged ahead as France's top scorer in the tournament.

Henry remained on the bench for the final group game versus Denmark as an already-qualified France rested several players. He returned to the starting line-up for a 1-0 win over Paraguay in France's first match of the knockout phase – a victory that brought them head to head with Italy in the quarter-finals.

Team: Barthez, Thuram, Blanc, Desailly, Lizarazu, Deschamps, Karembeu (65), Petit, Djorkaeff, Zidane, Guivarc'h (65)
Subs: Trezeguet (65), Henry (65)

Henry and France had progressed to the last eight of the tournament without setting the tournament alight, and ahead of their quarter-final against Italy some were wondering whether their opponents – one of the historical giants of international football – would be too strong for them.

Jacquet was sufficiently concerned to bring in a third defensive midfielder, Karembeu, alongside Deschamps and Petit, but that meant sacrificing an attacker. The victim of this tactical tweak was Henry, who dropped to the bench.

Henry had to wait until the 65th minute to enter the biggest game of his career so far, brought on with fellow substitute Trezeguet as Jacque attempted to convert France's superiority into victory. France had dominated the opening hour, with Zidane dictating the game, while Italy only had two first-half chances (both falling to Vieri and both saved by Barthez) to show for their efforts. To France's frustrations, the game went to extra time.

Despite obvious fatigue on both sides, the ensuing 30 minutes were not lacking in chances, with Italy's pony-tailed icon Baggio volleying a shot past the far post. With just 2 minutes left before a dreaded penalty shoot-out, Henry put Djorkaeff through with a lofted ball over the top, but he failed in his effort to lift the ball over onrushing Italian goalkeeper Pagliuca.

So it would come down to ten kicks to divide the two neighbouring nations and someone (there was always *someone* in a penalty shoot-out) destined to be forever tortured by their failure to cope with the intense pressure of what has been called 'the longest walk of a footballer's life'.

Zidane scored first for France, with Baggio responding for Italy. Next up was Lizarazu whose shot was saved, but Albertini fared no better. Trezeguet, the young sharp-shooter, showed his metal by scoring convincingly before Costacurta levelled things up for Italy. Then it was Henry's turn.

With the shoot-out tied at 2-2, Henry ambled from the half-way line to the penalty spot looking focused but relaxed, considering the colossal weight on his shoulders. His heart was doubtless racing at a million miles per hour, and yet at no point did he appear visibly fazed. He placed the ball on the spot, took several paces back and began his run-up. Reaching the ball, he side-footed it powerfully to the goalkeeper's left, evading his flailing hands and finding the net. Henry had held his nerve.

Vieiri responded by scoring for Italy and Blanc did the same with France's fifth penalty, leaving Di Biagio needing to put his kick away to keep Italy in the tie. His shot crashed against the crossbar and the Stade de France went wild.

'I was telling myself that this was the moment I had always dreamt of, but when everything could go wrong,' Henry later said about his penalty. 'To reassure myself, I told myself that Aimé Jacquet trusted me, that I wasn't an imposter.'

Henry's contribution to the victory amounted to less than 55 minutes, but more than any other game of the tournament it represented the often paper-thin line between success and failure. Struck a fraction lower and Pagliuca would almost certainly have saved and the courageous youngster who stepped up ahead of several more experienced teammates may have never recovered. Henry trod that precarious line with the same nimbleness he showed when dancing past opponents and he was now two games from becoming a world champion.

As is so often the case with narrow victories, France's win against Italy seemed to provide an injection of belief that created an unstoppable momentum. They went on to beat Croatia 2-1 in the semi-finals through sheer force of will before despatching Brazil 3-0 in the final to win the World Cup for the first time in the country's history.

Henry remained on the bench for both games, coming on as an early substitute against Croatia but not getting on the pitch at all in the final due to Desailly's sending off at 2-0 compelling France to shut up shop. But there would be no recriminations. For now at least, Henry was on top of the world.

As was hoped, France's victory brought the entire country together in celebration. In the centre of Paris, having rarely taken pride in its sporting stars, the French public greeted the victorious players with the kind of veneration normally reserved for returning war heroes. The Champs-Élysées was awash with beer and champagne as all races and social classes danced and drank in unison. Almost without exception, French people of a certain age would come to refer to that World Cup victory as the defining moment of their late twentieth century.

Years later, speaking to the journalist Amy Lawrence, Henry described what the moment meant to him:

A lot of amazing players never won the World Cup, so to do it at twenty, and have that medal in your bag, is a difficult feeling to explain. I don't think I will ever realise what happened during that World Cup. The day after the final, I was watching TV and saw on the Champs-Élysées guys in suites getting out of their Mercedes to party with total strangers dressed in their underwear, and letting them dance on their car bonnets too. I said to myself, 'it's fabulous to see Paris and the whole of France come together'.

Just out of his teens and with his name already etched permanently in French folklore, Henry was now faced with the task of ensuring the World Cup would not be the zenith of his career, but a lightning rod for greater things to come.

Lazio 1 Juventus 3
Serie A, 17 April 1999

There are several theories as to why, in the months following France's World Cup triumph, Henry failed to kick on and take his game to the next level as many had expected. Burnout was one guess, a common complaint among players deprived of a sustained off-season rest.

Another was that his head had been turned by serious interest from a number of major European clubs and that Monaco's refusal to sanction his release had caused him to sulk and lose his form.

Henry not only became an irregular presence in the Monaco team, but also lost his international place, despite finishing as France's top scorer at the World Cup. Indeed, after featuring as a substitute in their opening European Championships qualifier against Iceland, Henry did not win another cap for a staggering eighteen months, finding himself demoted to the Under-21s. The rollercoaster on which Henry had hurtled along for several years seemed to have careered off the track entirely.

In January 1999, halfway through the European domestic season, it was announced that Henry would be joining Italian club Juventus for £7 million on a four-and-a-half-year deal. One of the great institutions of world football, the Turin-based side already boasted three Frenchmen in Zidane, Deschamps and Blanchard, but were going through a turbulent period both on and off the pitch, and at the time Henry signed languished in mid-table.

Nevertheless, they still boasted several prestigious names, including Del Piero and Fonseca, and irrespective of his World Cup winner's medal, Henry would soon face the reality that he was now a small fish in a big pond and had plenty to prove.

After signing, Henry attempted to dampen down expectations. 'I'll play as I did at Monaco, on the wing, either on the left or the right. I'm not like David Trezeguet. People shouldn't expect bagfuls of goals from me.'

Henry made his Juventus debut against Perugia, coming on for the final 20 minutes of a 2-1 victory. He started the next game, but before he had even got his proverbial feet under the desk, the actual man behind the desk, Marcello Lippi, was fired and replaced by Carlo Ancelotti.

The managerial change actually worked in Henry's favour and he found himself getting more game time under the new coach. Juventus continued to struggle domestically, but were beating all before them in the Champions League, and by mid-March had progressed to the semi-finals, where they would meet Manchester United.

In the first leg at Old Trafford, Juventus were just seconds away from achieving a memorable victory, only to be denied by an equaliser at the death, and the two teams would meet again in the second leg two weeks later with the tie finely balanced. Between those two games was a league match at Lazio, who for much of the season had looked likely to coast to title success, but whose season had recently come off the boil.

Team: Peruzzi, Di Livio, Luliano, Ferrara, Mirkovic, Henry, Davids, Tacchinardi (78), Conte (88), Amoruso, Inzaghi (54)
Subs: Esnaider (54), Deschamps (78), Birindelli (88)

Even with Juventus in an unfamiliar mid-table position, the opportunity to claim the scalp of Italy's biggest club seemed to motivate Lazio and they began the first half with great attacking vigour, hitting the post and going close on a number of other occasions.

On 24 minutes, Henry opened the scoring for Juventus with a goal that owed as much to bad goalkeeping as any great skill on the Frenchman's part. Cutting inside from the left wing, Henry unleashed a powerful shot towards Marchegiani's near post. Despite its velocity, the shot was eminently saveable but the goalkeeper fumbled it terribly and allowed the ball to trickle into the net. It was Henry's first goal for Juventus since his January transfer and after an unconvincing start to his time in Italy he celebrated with commensurate glee.

Fourteen minutes later, Juventus doubled their lead through a cool finish from Amoruso and the away side went into the break with a convincing lead. Equally resounding had been Henry's performance, which saw him offer a permanent threat from the left that was capped by his opening (albeit fortunate) goal.

The second half saw Henry continue to attack Lazio with a confidence and verve that had hitherto been unseen since arriving in Turin. After Mancini pulled a goal back for Lazio with a fine header from a corner, Henry topped off his display by restoring Juve's two-goal advantage. Once again, there was an element of fortune about the goal, with the Lazio 'keeper spilling a free-kick straight out to Henry, who scored with a simple tap in.

But the truism that you make your own luck was never more apt. Henry had played what would be his finest game for Juventus, although ultimately it would not be enough for his time at the club to be remembered as anything but a disappointment. He finished the season having scored three goals in thirteen starts, and his failure to adapt to a wide role which required as much defensive responsibility as attacking, became the received wisdom for why he struggled in Italy.

Years later, however, in an interview with *FourFourTwo* magazine, Henry offered a different perspective:

> There's something that needs clearing up. People often say I didn't play much at Juve, but I always played. First of all, I only joined them in January, which explains the limited number of games. I played in all of the remaining sixteen games of the season, starting in thirteen of them; the first three I was on the bench because the coach, Marcello Lippi, was in the process of deciding to quit the club and thought it best to give me a bit of time. And in the last five or six games I either scored or set up a goal. One or the other. It's true that it took me a few games to get used to the system, because we played a 3-5-2 system I wasn't used to, but I soon adapted and started to play well. I left Juventus for other reasons, which I've never wanted to go into.

The nature of those 'other reasons' that were claimed to have been behind him leaving Juventus in August of 1999, just seven months after joining the club, remain unclear. But whatever the cause of his departure, the cloud under which he left Turin came with a significant silver lining. His ensuing move would come to define his career, and owed a debt to a chance meeting thousands of feet in the sky.

'Sometimes, destiny is weird,' Henry once said about the 'sliding doors' moment that changed his life forever. 'After the Juventus game at the end of the season I went back to Paris. And who was on the plane? The boss was on the plane. That is when I told him I would love to join Arsenal.'

The boss in question was Arsène Wenger, the man who gave Henry his debut at Monaco and a long-time admirer of a player he was convinced would end up as a striker, not a winger, as he had told him when the pair met a couple of years earlier.

'I won the World Cup as a winger,' Henry said. 'People all over the world recognised me as a winger. So for me it was kind of strange. I'd already been in the national team, and Arsène was telling me I could have another career as a centre-forward. It was difficult to understand.'

That game against Lazio, the stand-out 90 minutes of an otherwise forgettable phase of Henry's career, demonstrated the raw materials that would soon be honed to create arguably the world's greatest centre-forward. Henry would no longer find Wenger's prophecy difficult to understand.

Arsenal 2 Leicester City 1
Premier League
7 August 1999

In the summer of 1999, Arsenal fans were still coming to terms with having witnessed Manchester United achieve an unprecedented treble. By comparison, Arsenal's double success of 1998 was cast abruptly into distant memory, and, to make matters worse, one of their shining lights, the young and hugely gifted French striker Nicola Anelka, had finally forced a move away from the club following months of acrimony, joining Real Madrid for an eye-watering £23.5 million. The club record fee that Arsenal received was some consolation, but the overriding sense was disappointment that they had failed to retain one of the world's most talented young footballers.

Manager Arsène Wenger responded by bringing in reinforcements of contrasting credentials. Aged thirty-one, Davor Suker was a highly experienced Croatian international, who had enjoyed huge success in Spain, including winning both La Liga and the Champions League with Real Madrid. Despite being past his prime, and lacking the big-money price tag that many were craving, the signing gave some hope to supporters who felt spurned by Anelka's departure.

Wenger's other attacking addition was at first glance more curious, though perhaps not to those who had been observing his transfer dealings since arriving at the club in 1996. Two versatile French defenders, Emmanuel Petit and Gilles Grimandi, were graduates of Wenger's time as coach at AS Monaco and within a year of Wenger's appointment both had joined him at Highbury. While he would quickly gain a reputation for his revolutionary approach to football, Wenger was clearly also a man with an eye on the past.

One of Wenger' great young prodigies at Monaco had been a seventeen-year-old Thierry Henry, but despite already being a World Cup winner with France, his star had waned following his disappointing eight months at Juventus.

It was enough to provoke question marks when it was announced that the now twenty-one-year-old would become the third protégé to follow Wenger's path (via the scenic route) from the Cote d'Azur to north London. The fee, a club record £11.5 million, also seemed excessive to some given his Italian travails, but Wenger was undeterred. He saw in Henry enough potential to justify the gamble. Ahead of the season opener versus Leicester City at Highbury, Wenger said,

> He was the top scorer in the Under-17s for France when I first had him and I think that, as well as having the qualities of youth, pace and power, he is a good finisher. That is something he has not worked on enough in the last two years because he has played more wide, but I think he can become a central striker again. That is what we will try to develop together.

Team: Manninger, Dixon, Winterburn, Grimandi, Keown, Ljungberg (46), Vieira, Petit, Parlour (64), Bergkamp (90), Kanu
Subs: Henry (46), Overmars (64), Sylvinho (90)

The first 45 minutes of Arsenal's season passed by in forgettable fashion and, with the score locked at 0-0 at half-time, Arsène Wenger decided to introduce his record summer signing to the action.

Replacing the Swedish schemer Ljungberg, Henry trotted onto the Highbury turf wearing the No. 14 shirt that had been foisted upon him on arriving at the club (contrary to popular belief, he did not choose the shirt in homage to distinguished former wearers of the number such as Johan Cruyff). But before he'd even had a chance to show the fans his explosive turn of pace, Leicester took the lead when Cottee pounced at the far post with a simple tap in.

Arsenal responded like a team that could not afford an opening-day defeat in front of their home crowd and equalised after a misplaced defensive header fell into the path of Bergkamp, who finished sweetly.

The remaining 25 minutes were dominated by the home team, but Arsenal would need all of that time to force a winner, and when it arrived the eager debutant was heavily involved.

With 90 minutes on the clock, a Petit corner reached Henry, whose header was diverted into his own net by Sinclair. Henry wheeled away, more in hope than expectation that he would be credited with the goal, but his celebrations were jubilant nonetheless. He had given the fans a significant taste of his talents and helped secure a vital victory for his new team in the process.

For Arsène Wenger, there was reason for optimism, especially with Davor Suker, still awaiting a work permit and match-fitness, yet to integrate into the side. 'We needed the experience in the box of Suker,' he said after the match, 'but even without him we were much more dangerous with Henry on and Overmars on the flanks.'

The Leicester manager Martin O'Neill concurred. 'They were not devoid of options last year but they have even more this time. They have such strength in depth.'

As for Henry, on his first appearance for the club he had achieved precisely what every player at a new club wants: he'd made an impact.

Southampton 0 Arsenal 1
Premier League
18 September 1999

Following Arsenal's opening day win against Leicester, Arsène Wenger decided to promote Henry into the starting eleven for the next five league games. Results were mixed, with defeats to Manchester United and Liverpool before the month of August was out, and no-one was struggling more than Henry himself. Playing upfront, his lack of confidence was palpable and on the rare occasion he had a chance to score he snatched at it like a man too anxious to succeed.

Having for so long being exiled out on the wing at Monaco and Juventus, he now found himself having to go back to basics. 'It takes time to relearn how to move, to bend your run and find the right angle to score goals,' he would later say, admitting that during this period he 'doubted that [he] could impose myself as a centre-forward'.

His troubles were cast into an even less favourable light when Davor Suker came straight into the starting line up at home to Aston Villa and promptly scored two goals in a 3-1 victory. Henry was brought on as a late substitute but by that time the game was wrapped up and the following day's headlines had been written. 'Suker punch, Henry floored' may well have tempted the tabloid sub-editors, but the truth was that it was still far too early to judge a player who was still finding his feet at a new club in a new league.

When Arsenal travelled to Southampton in mid-September, Henry once again started on the bench as the team went in search of another victory that they hoped would get their league season back on track.

Team: Manninger, Dixon, Grimandi, Keown, Adams, Winterburn, Overmars (84), Ljungberg (46), Vieira, Kanu (71), Bergkamp
Subs: Parlour (46), Henry (71), Luzhny (84)

With defeats inflicted by two of their major rivals, the opening month of the season had provided little evidence that this was an Arsenal team capable of reclaiming the title they won in 1998. But following the previous league victory versus Aston Villa, another positive result at Southampton would provide much-needed momentum.

The first 25 minutes saw neither side looking likely to score, but as the half drew on Southampton began to impose themselves. With the score at 0-0, Wenger's half-time substitution of Parlour for Ljungberg seemed to betray the fact that Henry was not yet fully trusted as a dependable option. Yet when he did eventually get his chance with 19 minutes remaining, replacing Kanu, he was ordered to play upfront. If this was indeed a vote of confidence, Henry accepted it with impeccable grace.

The pendulum had already swung Arsenal's way by the time Henry made his entrance, but it was when Southampton defender Lundekvam was forced off injured that Arsenal – and Henry in particular – really began to turn the screw. Henry had only been on the pitch for 5 minutes when he raced onto a flick-on, leaving him well positioned to score, but he saw his shot blocked. Lundekvam's replacement Almeida was struggling to cope with Henry's pace, but the Frenchman was about to prove that he was no one-trick pony.

With 11 minutes left on the clock, Adams played a ball into Henry's feet on the edge of the penalty area. With his back to goal, he held off a defender before nudging the ball to his left. For a moment it appeared that he had pushed it too far, but in one fluid movement he stretched and unleashed a whipped shot that flew past the goalkeeper's outstretched hand and into the net.

The ball was hit with enough force to knock Henry off balance, but he was soon back on his feet, making his way to the celebrating Arsenal fans by the corner flag with his teammates in hot pursuit. On arrival, Henry placed a nonchalant hand on the flag and made a mock military salute before blowing a kiss to the jubilant supporters. It was a trademark celebration that he and teammate David Trezeguet had adopted at Monaco in honour of Argentine striker Gabriel Batistuta.

Yet despite the significance of the moment – not to mention the importance of the goal – Henry's expression remained unmoved. His reluctance to display overt happiness when he scored would become a regularly commented upon characteristic throughout his career, blamed on everything from a fierce self-critical streak to an inherently brooding personality to an overly demanding father. But this was no time for psychoanalysis. Henry had scored his first goal – a goal of exceptional quality – for Arsenal and with it won them the game.

Arsenal 2 Derby County 1
Premier League
28 November 1999

Despite his match-winning goal against Southampton, Henry remained on the bench for Arsenal's next game at home to Swedish club AIK Solna in the Champions League. In this case, 'home' meant Wembley Stadium, where Arsenal were temporarily playing their European games to allow more fans to attend than could do so at Highbury, which had almost half the capacity.

Appearing at the national stadium for the first time, Henry repeated the same trick as in the Southampton game, coming off the bench to score a late goal to put Arsenal ahead, this time with a controlled finish from just inside the box. Seconds later he set up Suker for a simple tap-in. He was rewarded with a starting berth in the following league game at home to Watford, with Kanu scoring the only goal in a 1-0 win.

For the next month, Henry either started matches or came off the bench, but results for the team remained inconsistent. The stand-out match came against Chelsea at Stamford Bridge where, with just 15 minutes left, Arsenal turned around a two-goal deficit to win in the final moments, courtesy of a sensational Kanu hat-trick. Henry had entered the fray with 25 minutes to go and while he contributed comparatively little to the comeback, it represented perhaps the first truly memorable match of his Arsenal career. However he had not yet been able to shrug off the consensus that he would never be a reliable finisher in front of goal.

Against Newcastle at Highbury in late October, Henry suffered an injury that would rule him out for almost a month. While it seemed like a blow at the time, Henry used his spell on the sidelines to work on his fitness.

At the end of November, Arsenal hosted Derby County and Henry returned to the starting line-up alongside Bergkamp in attack. It was another opportunity to prove that he deserved to be a regular fixture in the starting eleven and not just a 'wild card' option from the bench.

Team: Manninger, Luzhny, Adams, Upson, Parlour, Grimandi, Petit, Overmars (81), Henry (73), Bergkamp (64)
Subs: Kanu (64), Suker (73), Malz (81)

Arsenal lined up with Seaman, Dixon, Keown, Vieira and Ljungberg all missing through either injury or suspension and their absence was felt within just 2 minutes when the away team took the lead through Sturridge.

Sometimes conceding a goal can spark a team into life and on this occasion it seemed to have that very effect. Arsenal responded to the early set back by going straight on the attack and within minutes Henry went on a strong run only to stumble as he shot.

Arsenal were pressing hard for the equaliser and on 12 minutes it duly arrived. Overmars turned Delap neatly in the centre of the pitch and burst forward before releasing a pass for Henry to chase down the inside-left channel. To no one's surprise, he easily outpaced Carbonari and, albeit from a tight angle, found himself in on goal. Until that point, his short Arsenal career had shown no indication that inside Henry there was a top class finisher fighting to get out. But what happened next was perhaps the genesis of his evolution into the player he became. In mid-stride he almost effortlessly slotted the ball past Poom and inside the far post to put Arsenal back on level terms.

To an outsider, it was a proficient but unremarkable goal, but to those with a closer perspective, it felt like a turning point.

The ascendancy was now with Arsenal, and although they failed to force a second goal, there were plenty of positives to take into the half-time break. In particular the form of Henry, who had played with notable sharpness and vigour, topped off with a goal of real quality. But it was soon to get even better.

With just 6 minutes of the second half gone, Overmars once again picked the ball up from deep and made inroads into Derby territory. He cut infield and spotted Henry, who had pulled away to the right of his marker. Overmars slid a pass into Henry's feet, but by this time the defender had moved across and seemed to have cut out a direct route to goal. However, this was not accounting for Henry's combination of technique and pace. Opening out his body, Henry's first touch with his right foot instantly knocked the ball both forward and away from the retreating defender. His speed ensured he got to the ball first, and as the goalkeeper advanced Henry slotted the ball into the far corner of the net. Arsenal were ahead and Henry had his first brace for the club.

Soon after, Henry may well have got his hat-trick when Bergkamp played the ball across the penalty box, only for his own teammate Winterburn to get in his way.

With 17 minutes left, the substitutes' board went up and Henry was replaced by Suker. Highbury rose to its feet to applaud the efforts of a player who had finally proved he could show composure in front of goal. It was a pivotal moment for Henry and would provide the building blocks for the rest of the season. The fans now believed in him and, more importantly one sensed, Henry believed in himself.

Arsenal 2 Tottenham Hotspur 1
Premier League
19 March 2000

Following his brace against Derby in November, Henry had established himself as a regular in the starting line-up, scoring a creditable eleven goals in nine appearances along the way. By the time Tottenham came to visit Highbury for a league match that Arsenal had to win to revive their hopes of qualifying for the Champions League, Henry had notched fifteen goals in all competitions – just a couple short of Anelka's total for the entire previous campaign.

It was not just the number of goals that had impressed, but their quality and variety too. Indeed, one of them, against Deportivo La Coruna at Highbury in the UEFA Cup, even came from a header, perhaps the least impressive aspect of his game.

No longer were people debating whether he would ever be a consistent goalscorer. On the contrary, the question on everyone's lips ahead of his first ever north London derby (he had missed Arsenal's defeat at White Hart Lane the previous November through injury) was more often 'how good can he be?'

With Henry's stock rising fast, the Tottenham game offered another opportunity to spread the word, with the game being beamed back live to television viewers in his native France. The European Championships, to be co-hosted by Belgium and the Netherlands, was under three months away and one of the key discussions back home was over who should lead the attack for Les Bleus. At this rate, Henry had as good a claim as anyone.

Team: Manninger, Dixon, Luzhny, Adams, Sylvinho, Parlour, Vieira, Grimandi, Overmars (56), Henry (76), Kanu
Subs: Ljungberg (56), Winterburn (76)

It was Tottenham who started the game brighter and in the opening exchanges Ginola and Leonhardsen both went close with shots from distance. Arsenal, however, managed to take the lead after 20 minutes when Sylvinho whipped over a corner from the right and Henry beat a statuesque Spurs defence to the ball, flicking a near-post header off Armstrong and into the net for an own-goal.

Spurs nearly levelled in similar fashion soon after, but this time Sylvinho was on hand to hack Iversen's header off the line. The equaliser was not long in coming, however, as Ginola sent over a cross and Armstrong glanced an excellent header across Manninger and into the far corner.

The goal only served to fire Arsenal to more urgent probings. Deep into first-half stoppage time, Parlour was tripped by Taricco as he burst into the box and Henry stepped up to send Walker the wrong way for his sixteenth goal of the season (and his first penalty since arriving in English football).

Arsenal remained largely in control during the second half and with 14 minutes remaining Henry was replaced by the left back Winterburn as Arsène Wenger focussed on protecting his side's narrow lead.

As the game reached its final stages, Spurs found a late burst of attacking energy but Arsenal managed to hold on for a victory that took them back above Chelsea into fourth place in the Premiership.

While never quite setting the game on fire, Henry had done enough to earn the Man of the Match award thanks to his constant battling and impressive ball retention despite the close attentions of mountainous defender Sol Campbell. It was perhaps the first time that Henry looked to have fully acclimatised to the English game, both physically and mentally. He had also, quite clearly, enjoyed every second of it.

In his biography of Henry, Philippe Auclair recounts an interview the striker gave in the players' tunnel after the game:

> To play here is an extraordinary privilege. Even when you miss something, when you lose the ball, people don't boo, people clap. This was my first derby, and it is something truly extraordinary. The fans were red-hot. And that's what I love: people are aware that you've given everything you had in your guts. That's why I do things I wouldn't have attempted back in France, because the fans push me, and make you feel that you want to give everything for them.

Scotland 0 France 2
International Friendly
29 March 2000

Week by week Henry was adding to his blossoming reputation as one of the Premier League's most prodigious strikers, but it only served to add surprise to his continued exile from the French senior team, which now stretched to eighteen months.

The World Champions, now managed by Roger Lemerre, had stuttered through their Euro 2000 qualifying campaign, only narrowly avoiding a play-off thanks to a late winner by Trezeguet in their final match at home to Iceland.

Even stranger was the fact that since his appointment back in July 1998, Lemerre had come in for great criticism for his refusal to blood fresh talent. What better way to get the critics off his back than to select a twenty-two-year-old World Cup winner making significant waves in one of Europe's toughest leagues?

But Henry was becoming increasingly difficult to overlook. Seventeen goals for the season, including a Man of the Match performance at home to Tottenham in a game televised live in France, finally forced Lemerre's hand and Henry was named in his squad to face Scotland in a friendly at the end of March.

With just over two months until France's opening match of Euro 2000 against Denmark, Henry had been granted the opportunity to convince Lemerre that he deserved to be back playing for his country not just as a cameo, but for years to come.

Team: Rame, Thuram, Desailly, Blanc, Lizarazu, Ludovic, Giuly (46), Deschamps (60), Petit, Djorkaeff (46), Dugarry (72), Henry
Subs: Micoud (46), Wiltord (46), Vieira (60), Pires (72)

Henry was one of three Arsenal players to be included in the France squad for the friendly against Scotland, along with Patrick Vieira and Emmanuel Petit, as French football continued to reap the fruits of Arsène Wenger's virtual colonisation of the club.

A former Arsenal player, Anelka, who had become France's first-choice centre-forward during their Euro 2000 qualifying campaign, plus Henry's old Monaco teammate Trezeguet, were both left out as French coach Lemerre used the opportunity of a friendly match to assess the form of alternative candidates.

With France seeking their first ever victory on Scottish soil, it was the home side who made the early running in an exhilarating opening 15 minutes. But France slowly began to exert their superiority and at the hub of all of their good work was Henry, playing on the left of a front three and looking every inch a man with something to prove. Scotland held out until 9 minutes after half-time, when substitute Wiltord finished a lightning-quick France attack to shoot cleanly under the body of goalkeeper Sullivan.

By now France were toying with the Scots and never looked like surrendering their eleventh clean sheet in their last fourteen games. On the stroke of the final whistle, they wrapped up victory with a fine goal from Henry to complete a thoroughly satisfying return to the international scene.

Vieira surged forward with a trademark run from midfield and as he entered the penalty box a Scotland defender nicked the ball off his toes, only to see it trickle back outside the box where Henry was lurking. He calmly slotted a right-footed shot into the far corner of the net for his first goal for France since the 1998 World Cup.

In the relatively inconspicuous setting of a friendly at Hampden Park, Henry had reminded France what he had to offer with a performance of upmost excellence. No more would Henry be treated as surplus to requirements by his country – not for a long time, at least.

Arsenal 2 Chelsea 1
Premier League
6 May 2000

Arsenal went into their penultimate game of the league season against FA Cup finalists Chelsea knowing that victory would virtually assure them of automatic Champions League qualification. An impressive five wins in a row had not been enough to catch runaway leaders Manchester United, but a place at Europe's top table for the third year running would provide some consolation.

European football was still very much on the agenda in another sense, with Arsenal having progressed to the final of the UEFA Cup where they would play Turkish club Galatasaray in Copenhagen later in the month. The Gunners' Champions League campaign had ended at the group stage back in October, following a heavy defeat at Wembley to Barcelona, meaning they would parachute directly into the less prestigious European competition.

But before that, the focus was on finishing strongly in the league. For Henry, the Chelsea match also provided an opportunity to go head to head against his two French international teammates, Desailly and Leboeuf, both highly respected defenders and, like Henry, alumnis of the 1998 World Cup-winning squad.

Henry's form over the previous six months had already established him as one of the Premier League's most feared strikers and he went into the Chelsea match with twenty-three goals in all competitions to his name. Given that he had begun the season with most fans and pundits unsure even of his best position, his progress had been startling.

Team: Seaman, Dixon, Adams, Sylvinho, Parlour, Grimandi, Vieira, Petit (77), Overmars (46), Bergkamp (68), Henry
Subs: Winterburn (46), Kanu (68), Luzhny (77)

The disappointment felt by Arsenal's failure to keep pace with Man United had been somewhat softened by their overall commendable showing in the league and continued progress in the UEFA Cup that had already earned them a place in the final. Alongside those team milestones was the emergence over the season of Henry as a striker of the highest calibre. His fearsome pace had surprised no one, but the rate of his development into both a great goalscorer and a scorer of great goals simply could not have been foreseen.

If some defenders were still waking up to his ability, there was no such excuse for Chelsea's French duo Desailly and Leboeuf, who had been playing alongside Henry for the past two years for France. It provided an intriguing subplot for the penultimate game of the league season at Highbury.

On 21 minutes, Henry gave Arsenal the lead when Leboeuf failed to clear a long-ball. The Frenchman took the ball beyond the advancing De Goey and, finding himself at a wide angle, turned back and brought the ball infield before slotting it home to put Arsenal 1-0 up.

With half-time approaching, Henry picked up his seventh caution of the season when he was penalised for a foul on Leboeuf. Henry responded by chucking the ball to the ground in anger and there followed a yellow card. Henry's occasional displays of petulance were perhaps a sign of his growing confidence in expressing himself on the pitch, but for fans who had been brought up on the misdemeanours of serial offender Ian Wright, there would be few complaints. An Arsenal legend, Wright was Arsenal's record goalscorer and Henry, who had become a keen student of the club's history, was well aware of his legacy.

In between studies, Henry was also busy building his own Arsenal backstory. As well as their volume, the sheer variety of his goals was beginning to receive plaudits and just a minute into the second half, he added another to his burgeoning repertoire. Bergkamp played a pass into the inside left channel and Henry picked it up and ran straight at Desailly. The defender tried to shepherd Henry onto his outside, but Henry muscled his way beyond him before sliding the ball under De Goey from a tight angle to extend Arsenal's lead.

It was perhaps the moment that Henry turned from a boy to a man in an Arsenal shirt. His sheer brute strength in holding off a man-mountain like Desailly was startling and it alerted people to the fact that he was not just a talented footballer but a true athlete.

The final whistle sounded to leave Arsenal five points clear in second place, with the small matter of the UEFA Cup final to play in eleven days' time. The League title may have eluded them, but the season had offered plenty of room for optimism. Now their task was to crown it with silverware.

Galatasaray 0 Arsenal 0
(Gala Won on Penalties)
UEFA Cup Final
17 May 2000

The league season had finished with a 3-3 home draw against Sheffield Wednesday (Henry scoring his 17th league goal of the season) leaving Arsenal in second place five points from their nearest challengers Leeds but a whopping eighteen from Man United, who had blown away the rest of the field in retaining their title.

Arsenal's poor showing in the Champions League had proved they also had a lot to learn on the European front, but luckily the UEFA Cup had provided them with succour and they had beaten some high calibre teams on the way to the final, where they would meet Turkish club Galatasaray at the Parken Stadium in Denmark.

The build-up to the match was overshadowed by sporadic riots across the city between Arsenal and Galatasaray fans. Rumours abounded that supporters of Leeds United had travelled to Copenhagen under the guise of being Arsenal fans to seek revenge for the fatal stabbing of two Leeds fans in Istanbul the previous month, but this was never proven. In any case, the footballing affiliations of the rioters in Copenhagen seemed a moot point.

Back on the pitch, it was a chance for Arsenal to secure their first European trophy since the UEFA Cup Winners' Cup in 1994 when they beat Italian club Parma 1-0. By coincidence, that game had also been played at Copenhagen's Parken Stadium and fans making the return trip did so with warm memories.

As for Henry, callow though he was in English football, it was easy to forget that he had already made a significant mark on the European stage with Monaco, having scored four goals in their 1997/98 Champions League campaign. Add to that a World Cup-winners medal with France and seven goals along Arsenal's European journey to Denmark and the sum total was a player of international pedigree. Could he now add his first trophy for Arsenal to his credentials?

Team: Seaman, Dixon, Keown, Adams, Sylvinho, Parlour, Petit, Vieira, Overmars (115), Bergkamp (75), Henry
Subs: Kanu (75), Suker (115)

Cup finals are typically cagey affairs, at least until the first goal is scored, but on this occasion both teams created chances throughout the match, but somehow the score remained 0-0.

With the deadlock unbroken, the game entered extra time and within minutes the match swung in Arsenal's favour when Hagi was sent off for the Turks after punching Adams on the back following a fairly innocuous tussle.

It seemed inevitable that the goal would come, but a succession of gilt-edged chances were missed, most notably by Henry, who had several shots saved by Galatasaray's Brazilian goalkeeper Taffarel and saw another fly across the goalmouth. Henry also created a good chance for Overmars, but his shot went wide and the game moved with increasing inevitably towards a penalty shoot-out.

There was still time for one final chance to go begging and Henry again was the culprit. A perfect cross found him unmarked in the penalty box and, as he rose to meet it, the goal that would have given Arsenal victory thanks to the 'Golden Goal' rule seemed assured. But despite being at virtual point-blank range, his powerful header was parried away by Taffarel.

Years later, Arsène Wenger said that Henry had the ability to be a great header of the ball but simply 'didn't fancy it much'. Indeed, it was generally acknowledged by his coaches that it was the one area of his game that he neglected. Perhaps with a little more diligence he could have won Arsenal the trophy.

With his header saved, penalties beckoned and as the final whistle went, both managers gathered their troops on the side of the pitch to decide on their five respective takers. A toss of the coin meant the kicks would be taken at the end of the Galatasaray fans which, given their reputation as some of the most vociferous in the world, afforded them an instant advantage.

Henry would almost certainly have stepped up to take one of Arsenal's spot-kicks but was forced off with an injury just 5 minutes before the end of extra-time. As it turned out, Arsenal missed the first two of their three penalties, leaving Galatasaray needing only to score four to win the game. They converted them all, securing the trophy and leaving Arsenal crestfallen. Adding salt to the wounds, the scorer of Galatasaray's winning penalty was Popescu – a former Tottenham player.

It also made it an unwanted hat-trick of penalty shoot-out defeats in cup competitions for Arsenal that season, having gone out of the FA Cup at Leicester and the Worthington Cup at Middlesbrough on spot-kicks.

As for Henry, the disappointment took a certain gloss off of what had been a magnificent debut season. It also allowed the view that Henry did not perform when it really mattered – and in particular in Cup finals – to germinate.

France 3 Denmark 0
European Championships Group Match, 11 June 2000

By the time the 2000 European Championship finals, which were being co-hosted by Holland and Belgium, came about, Henry's evolution into a bona fide centre-forward was complete, for Arsenal at least. For his national side, he was used either on the left or right of a front three, with one of Anelka or Trezeguet spearheading the attack.

Henry may have forged himself a regular berth in the France side after his surprising eighteen-month demotion to the Under-21s, but he still had some way to go before he was held in the same esteem by the French public as he was by his adoring Arsenal fans.

After all, this was a French team still riding the wave of their World Cup victory two years earlier, pumped with new-found self-confidence and boasting, in Zidane, a player considered by many to be the greatest of his generation. Henry may have been the main man at Highbury but his former teammate at Juventus still had a firm grip of that mantle for France.

Their opening match of the tournament would be against Denmark at the Jan Breydel Stadium in Bruges, with Henry and Djorkaeff lining up either side of Anelka at the tip of France's attacking trio. Henry had come a long way since that magical day at the Stade de France two years earlier. Now it was time to show just how far.

Team: Barthez, Thuram, Desailly, Blanc, Lizarazu, Deschamps, Petit, Zidane, Djorkaeff (52), Anelka (82), Henry
Subs: Vieira (52), Wiltord (82)

It was not long until France gained the ascendancy, and on 17 minutes they took the lead through an unlikely source. Henry played in Anelka and as he tried to take the ball past Schmeichel the goalkeeper dived at his feet, only to see it squirm out to a lurking Blanc, who calmly sidefooted home.

The remainder of the first half saw the French create chance after chance, and 6 minutes before half-time Henry, who had been a constant threat down France's left, thundered towards goal before squeezing in a shot that went marginally wide.

The second period continued in a similar vein, with France making most of the running. But it was not until the 64th minute that they forced a second goal, and this came from the increasingly influential Henry.

Just a minute earlier he had hit an inch-perfect cross from the left that Anelka looked certain to convert but somehow headed off target. Within 60 seconds, Henry had shown him the way with a goal that illustrated the completeness of the player he had now become.

A clipped pass from Zidane found Henry thundering down the inside left channel and despite Denmark defenders in pursuit there was no catching him. Henry entered the box before opening out his body and slotting the ball powerfully into the far corner past the helpless Schmeichel, who did not even attempt a dive.

France (and Henry in particular) were suddenly rampant. On 76 minutes, Henry was off again and only a challenge by Colding on the goal line stopped him from pulling it across for one of three waiting blue shirts.

Two minutes into injury time, France added a shine to their victory with a third goal when Vieira set up Wiltord for an easy finish.

It wrapped up a perfect start to the tournament for France, who were already showing signs of taking their game to even greater heights than two years earlier. And at the hub of this souped-up iteration was Henry, who, for the first time on the international stage, looked a player content in his own skin and in the blue shirt of France.

13

France 2 Italy 1
European Championships Final
2 July 2000

France were now just one victory away from becoming the first international side to win a World Cup and European Championship back-to-back. The last obstacle between them adding to their legacy of greatness was Italy, whose impregnable defence had virtually carried them to the final.

Henry's maturation into a vital cog in the French machine had been demonstrated by two Man of the Match performances and three goals, including a vital equaliser against Portugal in the semi-finals. Now a guaranteed starter when fit, at various points throughout the tournament he had been selected by coach Roger Lemerre to play across the entire width of the French frontline. But wherever on the pitch he was positioned, he was a persistent danger and main reference point for their attacks.

He had also struck up an impressive partnership with Real Madrid striker Anelka, despite uncertainty over the duo's suitability to play together. Yet, in three of France's five matches on their route to the final, they had done just that, most notably against Portugal, where they combined for Henry's crucial equaliser.

In France's quarter-final against Spain, it had been Zidane who enthralled with a second half performance of ingenuity and poise. But while Zidane remained the conductor of the French orchestra, Henry was the perfect concertmaster, ably supported by several fellow scholars from the 1998 World Cup-winning side.

Indeed, of the eleven players to finish that year's final against Brazil, eight would start against Italy two years later at the De Kuip Stadium in Rotterdam. Little wonder that confidence and belief raced through this side of proven winners. Now they had to harvest that self-assurance to produce another trophy.

Team: Barthez, Thuram, Desailly, Blanc, Lizarazu (86), Vieira, Deschamps, Djorkaeff (76), Zidane, Henry, Dugarry (58)
Subs: Wiltord (58), Trezeguet (76), Pires (86)

France coach Lemerre chose to start with Henry as his lone frontman, omitting Anelka despite them having teamed up well in three of France's matches so far. He instead opted for a 4-2-3-1 formation, with Henry at the tip of the attack and Dugarry, Zidane and Djorkaeff playing behind.

The opening half saw France stifled by Italy's resilient midfield shield, with Zidane given absolutely no space to work his magic and the supply lines to Henry virtually cut out. But on the few occasions the Arsenal man received the ball he created opportunities, including hitting the post in the opening minutes and then forcing fouls after excellent solo runs down the inside left.

At the break, France altered their tactics, with Zidane moving further forward, but it was Henry who remained the main danger. Four minutes into the second period he left a trail of Italian defenders in his wake before flashing a centre across the face of goal, which Zidane touched but could not turn in.

It was enough to force Italy into a change, replacing Fiore with Del Piero, and his link up with Totti galvanised Italy almost instantly. Three minutes after the substitution, Totti received the ball with his back to goal and played an impudent back-heel to free Pessotto on the right. His perfect cross found Delvecchio, who shot high past Barthez from 6 yards.

Del Piero then squandered a glorious chance to give Italy a two-goal lead, spurring France into an immediate substitution, with the struggling Dugarry withdrawn in place of Wiltord (who would join Henry at Arsenal that summer).

Henry still looked France's best hope of forcing an equaliser, and Toldo came to the rescue again, plunging bravely at his feet after 68 minutes. With time running out, France went for broke and brought on Trezeguet for Djorkaeff, meaning they now had three strikers on the pitch – four including Zidane, who had migrated even further forward as France's efforts became ever more frantic.

With the game entering injury time, Italy looked to have held out, but with 1 minute remaining, France embarked on one final attack. A long ball was headed on to Wiltord, who controlled it instantly with his chest. Running onto his own knock down, Wiltord unleashed a powerful left-foot shot that crept under the left hand of Toldo and nestled in the far corner.

France had saved themselves at the death and the game went into extra time, with the newly introduced 'Golden Goal' format meaning that the next goal would win the trophy – or a penalty shoot-out would decide it.

Four minutes into extra time, Toldo denied French substitute Pires (like Wiltord, soon to become a teammate of Henry at Arsenal), sustaining a bloody nose in the process. But 9 minutes later, the game was won and it was Pires at the heart of the move.

Picking up the ball in the left hand channel, he beat two Italians before cutting the ball back to Trezeguet, who launched a thunderbolt strike with his left boot to beat Toldo and give France a dramatic victory.

The French players, many of whom had shared each other's joy on the Stade de France pitch two years earlier, had shown that their World Cup victory was no fluke. By following it up with another major tournament success, they had become the high-water mark of France's football history.

For Henry, another Man of the Match award in the final as well as finishing France's top scorer (as he did in 1998) meant that he could no longer be considered a peripheral figure as an international footballer. From now on, Henry would wear the blue of France with an authority he had earned.

Arsenal 1 Manchester United 0
Premier League
1 October 2000

Following his stellar first season at Arsenal that led seamlessly into his performances for France at Euro 2000, Henry experienced a comparatively quiet start to the next campaign. Four goals in ten games was a respectable return, but he had not yet hit the heights that fans had come to expect and he went into Arsenal's home game with Man United having failed to find the net in nearly a month. In reference to Henry, *The Guardian* writer David Lacey wrote that 'a striker without goals becomes a little lost, like a dog that has forgotten where it has buried a bone'.

Nonetheless, Arsenal had won all five of their home games in all competitions so far and were in relatively good shape, despite lining up without any of their summer signings in the starting eleven. Indeed, only one of them – French striker-cum-winger and club record signing Wiltord – was even on the bench. Another, Pires, who had bolstered Arsenal's French contingent to six, had not appeared in any of the previous three games and had not yet fully acclimatised to the English game. To make matters worse, talismanic French midfielder Vieira was completing the last of a five-game suspension following two red cards in the opening two matches of the season.

But irrespective of personnel, this was a match that Arsenal could little afford to lose, having already fallen three points behind the champions by the time they came to Highbury. Even at this stage of the season, dropping six behind would begin to appear ominous, particularly with the spectre of Man United's runaway title success the previous season still hanging in the air.

Team: Seaman, Keown, Adams, Sylvinho, Grimandi, Luzhny, Ljungberg, Parlour, Bergkamp (78), Kanu (57), Henry
Subs: Vivas (57), WIltord (78)

The rivalry that had built up between Arsenal and Manchester United in recent years meant that each clash between the two clubs generated Ali *v.* Foreman-esque levels of anticipation, and the games often lived up to their billing. Other times, the sheer pressure of the occasion meant that neither team played with the fluidity for which they were renowned, and the opening exchanges suggested this match would be the latter type.

In the opening half-hour, Henry's performance had been as insipid as anyone's and nothing pointed towards this being a game to remember. But then came a goal that would imprint itself on the memories of football fans everywhere.

It arrived when Beckham was cautioned for a foul on Ljungberg and Kanu tapped the resulting free kick to Grimandi, who played the ball into the feet of Henry with his back to goal. Instead of bringing it under control, Henry's first touch was to flick it up with his left foot before swivelling to volley with his right, sending the ball soaring through the air, over his former Monaco teammate and international colleague Barthez and into the top corner. It would not be the last time Henry would leave the French goalkeeper looking forlorn at Highbury.

Henry turned and ran directly to the dug-out, where he mimicked a popular television advertisement for the alcoholic drink Budweiser, putting an imaginary mobile phone to his ear and screaming the advert's 'Wassap!' catchphrase into the face of his applauding (and possibly confused) manager.

The pop-culture reference was not to everyone's taste, but there was no disagreement about the quality of the goal. It would be one thing to attempt something like that in a casual training session, but to do so in a tense match against one of your biggest rivals – and succeed – was quite another. As much as he was known for his sullen on-pitch persona, Henry was a player who simply loved to entertain. To borrow a phrase from his homeland, moments like this were his *raison d'être*, or at least his *raison d'jouer*.

After the match, Wenger would offer a more simple explanation for Henry's decision to shoot from such an unorthodox position:

> When you haven't been scoring goals, sometimes you need to try something a little bit crazy, something you don't have to think about but just do it. Thierry played with much more freedom once he had scored.

The rest of the half elapsed with relatively little incident, almost as if the players were keen to get back into the dressing room to discuss what they'd just witnessed and perhaps catch a replay on television.

But by the start of the second half, Man United regained their composure and Giggs soon tested Seaman's reflexes with a powerful shot. Yet as the game progressed, it was Arsenal who began to press forward and with an hour gone, Sylvinho went on a weaving run that took him into the Man United area, where he took the ball around Barthez only to find himself too wide to shoot on target.

Late in the game, as Man United went searching for the equaliser, Arsenal capitalised on the extra space and Henry had a chance to score his second after out-running United's defence, only for Barthez to rush out and deny him with a sliding tackle.

The final whistle went and Arsenal had secured a vital victory that narrowed the gap at the top of the table and propelled Henry back into the spotlight, thanks to a goal that would be talked about with wide-eyed wistfulness for years to come.

Arsenal 1 Liverpool 2
FA Cup Final
12 May 2001

The 2001 FA Cup final was the first of six to be played at the Millennium Stadium in Cardiff while Wembley was being rebuilt and it was Arsenal and Liverpool who had earned the privilege to play in that year's showpiece match.

A week before the final, Arsenal had ensured finishing in the top three of the Premiership, providing some consolation for their failure to present any kind of challenge to runaway leaders Man United (who in February had asserted their credentials in the strongest terms by trouncing Arsenal 6-1 at Old Trafford). Their Champions League campaign, too, ended in disappointment at the quarter-final stage when they were beaten by Valencia.

For Henry's part, his twenty-two goals up to April had been a strong showing for his second season in England – often a time when players experience a dip due to opponents becoming aware of their abilities. But he was still yet to win anything for the club and the Cup final represented his last chance of ending the season with silverware. Arsenal's 1998 double success had been heralded by many as the start of a dynasty, but that prediction would begin to appear foolhardy in the face of another trophy-less season.

Their opponents, Liverpool, had brought to an end their own three-year drought in February, beating Birmingham City in the Worthington Cup final (the first English final to be played at the Millennium Stadium) and were on course to win an historic Cup treble, with the FA Cup final being followed four days later with their appearance in the UEFA Cup final against Spanish club Alaves.

But Liverpool's reputation as one of the English football's foremost clubs had faded since the 1980s and Arsenal were now considered by most observers to be the more formidable side. Although Arsenal's trophy-winning credentials had slipped, with four of their regular starters (Henry, Pires, Vieira and Wiltord) all mainstays of a French side that were reigning World and European champions, they benefited from a kind of reflected aura of greatness, the mere presence of such decorated players unnerving opposing teams.

Liverpool, nonetheless, boasted their own match-winners, most notably England's Michael Owen, whose career had shared a notable parallel with Henry, having burst onto the scene at the 1998 World Cup, and who in six months would become the first Englishman to be named European Footballer of the Year since Kevin Keegan in 1978.

Team: Seaman, Dixon (90), Keown, Adams, Cole, Pires, Grimandi, Vieira, Ljungberg (90), Wiltord (76), Henry
Subs: Parlour (76), Kanu (85), Bergkamp (90)

Arsène Wenger's only real selection dilemma ahead of the final was whether to reinstall Bergkamp after a lengthy spell out through injury, or retain Wiltord, who had benefited from the Dutchman's absence. Wenger opted for the latter, pairing Henry upfront with his compatriot who had joined the club along with Pires after France's Euro 2000 success the previous summer.

After 16 minutes, Arsenal had their appeals for a penalty waved away and replays showed they had every right to be furious. Ljungberg released Henry, who skipped around Liverpool goalkeeper Westerveld, only for his shot to be saved by the arm of defender Henchoz, who had raced back to cover on the goal-line. Had the officials spotted the offence, a penalty would almost certainly have been accompanied by a red card for Henchoz.

With Liverpool playing mainly on the counter-attack, Arsenal were dominating possession but aside from Henry's chance were unable to breach Liverpool's defence and half-time came with the score deadlocked.

Liverpool had a narrow escape after 56 minutes when Henry juggled the ball past Westerveld, leaving Cole with the easiest of chances as the ball ran loose but his stabbed shot was cleared off the line. Arsenal scented a goal and with 19 minutes left their pressure finally told when Pires played in Ljungberg, who rounded the Liverpool goalkeeper and finished with aplomb.

Victory should have been assured almost immediately, only for Westerveld to make a point blank save from Henry. It was a miss that Arsenal would end up ruing.

With 8 minutes remaining, a McAllister free-kick from out on the left was not dealt with by the Arsenal defence, and as the ball bobbled in the box, Owen lashed a right-footed shot that arrowed into the corner with Seaman stranded.

Five minutes later and Liverpool's comeback was complete. Substitute Berger played a ball over the top for Owen to chase and after his pace

took him past Adams and Dixon he launched a precise left-footed shot that evaded Seaman's grasping hand and nestled in the far corner.

The final whistle went and Arsenal had acquired the unwanted record of losing a major Cup final twice in two seasons. But while they had failed to perform in the previous year's defeat to Galatasaray in the UEFA Cup, on this occasion they had controlled the match for almost the entire 90 minutes. Neither scenario let Arsenal fans feeling any better.

In Henry's view, despite notching an impressive forty-six goals in his first two seasons at the club, a key component was missing that would help push Arsenal over the line in their pursuit of silverware. 'We need a player who will be a fox in the box and on the pitch,' he said, after the final defeat,

We need a player like Owen is for Liverpool. I make a lot of runs and get wide a lot, but Owen is always in the box and we need someone like that. When I make wide runs and put in crosses there is often no-one there to put the ball in the net. Owen was the hero because he is always in the right place. We need a goalscorer like that.

16

Arsenal 3 Manchester United 1
Premier League
25 November 2001

By the time the 2001/02 season came around, Arsenal and Manchester United were well established as the dominant forces in English football. Matches between them were often epic affairs and the midfield rivalry between Vieira and Keane in particular provided each clash with a volcanic subplot.

Arsenal had been busy in the transfer market that summer in their efforts to wrestle the title back from Man United after three years of finishing runners-up to Alex Ferguson's side. By far the most high-profile arrival was England defender Sol Campbell, who had done the unthinkable and left Tottenham for their bitter rivals on a free transfer. Arsenal fans rejoiced in the capture of one of the world's best centre-backs and their satisfaction was doubled by the torment it caused supporters of their north London neighbours.

Despite the raft of new signings, Arsenal struggled for consistency throughout the autumn and went into their league match at home to Man United on the back of a disappointing Champions league defeat against Deportivo La Coruna in Spain. One player that no one could blame for Arsenal's disjointed form was Henry, who had already scored fifteen goals that season, including nine in his previous eight games.

He also had the memory of his sensational winning goal against Man United at Highbury the previous season. On that occasion, United goalkeeper and Henry's French teammate Barthez was left rooted to the spot as the ball sailed into the top corner. Now they would meet again. Would Barthez get his revenge by shutting out Henry and Arsenal, or could the home team revive their title challenge with victory?

Team: Taylor, Lauren, Campbell, Upson, Cole, Pires (83), Parlour, Vieira, Ljungberg, Henry, Kanu (64)
Subs: Bergkamp (64), Grimandi (83)

If there's one thing that managers try to drill into their players, it is the importance of starting games well. This is particularly important in games against strong opposition with statistics proving that the first goal in such games is often crucial.

Arsenal took heed of such advice and before long had tested Barthez on several occasions, including from two Henry free-kicks. But on this occasion, their early pressure counted for nothing and it was Man United who took the lead against the run of play when Silvestre's low cross was turned in by Scholes.

But instead of putting Man United on the front foot, the goal only served to reinforce Arsenal's dominance and when half-time arrived they could consider themselves unlucky to be going in behind. Their pressure continued after the break and within three minutes of the restart the equaliser had come. Pires found Ljungberg 25 yards out and the Swede took one touch before chipping the ball over Barthez.

With the rain teaming down, Arsenal found themselves camped out on the edge of United's box and it was only valiant defending from the away side that kept the score at 1-1. The minutes ticked by and it increasingly appeared that an enthralling game would end in deadlock. But then came ten farcical minutes that would live long in the memory.

On 80 minutes, Parlour took an ambitious potshot from distance, hitting a United defender on the edge of the box. As Barthez prepared to clear the ball upfield, Ljungberg quickly closed in on him and, in a moment of panic, the French goalkeeper rushed his clearance and miskicked it straight to the feet of Henry just outside the box. Henry's control was instant and he advanced into the box and slotted the ball past Barthez to give Arsenal a precious lead with just 5 minutes remaining.

Henry ran directly past his compatriot in celebration and cheekily turned back to give him a brief glance before lifting his shirt above his head in front of Arsenal's exuberant fans. Barthez stuck his tongue out in disbelief – a look that did nothing to assuage his humiliation. He had handed the game to Arsenal on a plate and consigned himself to being the butt of jokes at French international get-togethers for years to come.

But incredibly, it was about to get even worse for Barthez. With 5 minutes left, Vieira played a long ball over the top for Henry to chase, but the goalkeeper had anticipated it and left his line to collect. Barthez narrowly reached the ball first and the danger looked over, but, perhaps unnerved by what had happened five minutes earlier, he spilled it and Henry collected the loose ball, composed himself and finished into an empty net.

It was sheer joy for Arsenal and abject shame for one of the great goalkeepers of the era, who compounded his ignominy once again, this time by yanking his shorts up his thighs in frustration and providing the next day's newspapers with their back-page splash.

The victory delivered a huge fillip to Arsenal, who would only lose one more league game for the rest of a season that would end with Henry's first trophies for the club. And as much as any, it was this match and Henry's winning goals that would be remembered as the moment the tide turned in their favour.

17

Arsenal 3 Aston Villa 2
Premier League
9 December 2001

Arsenal had followed up their thrilling late victory against Manchester United at Highbury with two more excellent results, both featuring goals from Henry. He scored the second, a penalty, in a 2-0 win at Ipswich Town in the league and then, three days later, Henry's former team Juventus travelled to London for a vital Champions League clash that Arsenal had to win to maintain a realistic hope of progressing in the competition.

After his fruitless spell at the Turin club, it proved to be a therapeutic experience for Henry, who scored a fabulous free kick as Arsenal steamrollered Juventus in a hugely impressive 3-1 victory. It set them up well for the next challenge a few days later – a home league match with Aston Villa and another chance to add momentum to their rejuvenated title assault and make ground on Liverpool who had opened up a six-point lead at the top.

Indeed, by the time the game kicked off, Arsenal were fourth in the table, lagging behind not only Liverpool but Newcastle and Leeds too, who had all won their earlier matches that weekend. Even Aston Villa themselves were just two points behind Arsenal, giving the match at Highbury added significance.

The game would also be played against the backdrop of a crucial moment in Arsenal's history, as that same evening Islington Council would vote on whether to allow the club to build a new stadium on the site of Ashburton Grove, located a mere wayward Henry free kick away from Highbury.

Team: Taylor, Lauren, Campbell, Upson (45), Cole, Ljungberg (45), Parlour, Vieira, Pires, Henry, Bergkamp (67)
Subs: Keown (45), Wiltord (45), Kanu (67)

Arsenal's midweek exertions against Juventus had clearly taken their toll and they started the match with a surprising air of frailty. Their attacks lacked purpose and for the opening 20 minutes Aston Villa kept them at bay with relative ease. Then an Arsenal old boy came back to haunt them.

Despite having played under Wenger, Paul Merson was very much a relic of the 'old' Arsenal, when steak and chips rather than chicken and steamed vegetables were staples on the pre-match menu. He had left Arsenal in 1997, cruelly stuck on 99 goals for the club, but he would still get to have a final say at Highbury.

With 21 minutes gone, Enckelman, playing in goal in the absence of the injured Schmeichel, launched a huge kick upfield. Dublin headed on and Merson deftly lifted the ball over Arsenal goalkeeper Talyor from 9 yards. 'The immutable law of the ex' was how the journalist Brian Glanville famously described the habit of players scoring against their former team, but there was more at stake on this occasion than retribution.

Villa went further ahead in the 34th minute when Stone pounced on a loose ball to drive a low shot past Taylor. Arsenal were shaken and at half-time Wenger took the unusual measure of making two half-time substitutions, bringing on Keown for Upson and Wiltord for Ljungberg. The move instantly paid dividends.

Just a minute after the restart, Wiltord showed great reactions to volley a Parlour cross home with his left foot, putting Arsenal back into the game with a full half still to play. Arsenal were soon piling forward relentlessly, knowing that even a draw would not be satisfactory.

With 20 minutes to play, Vieira dispossessed Samuel on Villa's right and looked up to spot Henry lurking in the middle. With the ball bouncing at knee-height and a Villa defender in close attendance, Henry had plenty to do. He athletically jumped and brought the ball down in one movement and waited for the goalkeeper to make his move. Enckelman held his nerve, but that happened to be Henry's forte too. Henry steadied himself, weighed up his options and spotting a gap to the goalie's right slid the ball under his outstretched arm and into the corner.

Despite the disappointment of letting slip a two-goal lead, Villa stayed firm. The minutes passed and Arsenal's efforts to force a winner were in vain. But as the game entered injury time, a loose ball fell between Pires and Boateng and everyone watching would have put their money on the combative Villa midfielder coming out on top. But against all odds, Pires chose this moment to win one of the only fifty-fifty challenges of his career – and what a time to do it.

Looking up, Pires was confronted with two options. Kanu came short for the pass, but behind him Henry had already turned on the after-burners. It was a no-brainer. Pires slid a perfectly weighted ball between the Villa defence and Henry was on to it like a flash. So perfect was the pass that he didn't even need to take a touch and, as Enckelman advanced, Henry slotted the ball home to complete a dramatic, last minute comeback.

After the match, Arsène Wenger talked about his side exercising the demons of the last couple of years:

> With the Cup final [the previous year against Liverpool, which Arsenal lost] and the championship recently, the players had begun to believe that there was a pattern of us finishing second. The players want to be first and they believe they can win it. They showed their character, energy and desire to get on top against Villa. For us, it was a crucial game because Liverpool and Leeds also won. It's very tight at the top and don't write off Manchester United, who have the talent, a history of success and the money to buy.

But all the money in the world would not be able to purchase Henry right now. Arsenal had one of the world's finest footballers leading their title charge and if any clubs were considering trying their luck, they would have to wait. At least until Arsenal's new stadium plans, which were given the green light that night by Islington Council, would begin to take their toll on the club's financial strength. But that was a dilemma for another day.

Arsenal 1 Newcastle United 3
Premier League
18 December 2001

When Newcastle came to Highbury for a vital league match in mid-December, they did so having failed to win in their previous twenty-nine visits to London. Ahead of the game there were few willing to predict that the run was about to end.

Not that this was a bad Newcastle side. On the contrary, under the leadership of the venerable Bobby Robson (who would receive a Knighthood the following year), they were a team rejuvenated and had shown signs that season of being capable of a credible title challenge. Indeed, they arrived at Highbury knowing that victory by a two-goal margin would put them top.

For Arsenal, the need for a win was arguably even greater. In contrast with Newcastle, their fans did not only expect them to be fighting for the title, they demanded it. With their next two games being against Liverpool and Chelsea, a win here seemed vital.

Arsenal lined up with something approaching a first choice starting eleven, save for Taylor in goal who was continuing to deputise for Arsenal's first and second choice duo Seaman and Wright, both of whom were injured. Upfront, Henry lined up alongside Kanu, with Wiltord supporting from wide.

Team: Taylor, Lauren, Campbell, Keown, Cole, Parlour, Vieira, Pires, Henry, Kanu (45), Wiltord (67)
Subs: Van Bronckhorst (45), Bergkamp (67)

A game that was billed as a top-of-the-table clash between two in-form sides would ultimately be remembered as much for a number of unsavoury incidents and some highly dubious refereeing as the eventual result.

A strong opening spell for Arsenal led to them taking the lead, with Henry playing an unconventional role in the goal. Lauren's deep free-kick was flicked on by Kanu and Henry collected the ball on the edge of the box. He tried to work a shooting chance but the close attentions of a Newcastle defender forced him wide. From such a position, a less imaginative player would have passed conservatively to a teammate, but Henry had other ideas, flicking the ball up and launching himself into an acrobatic overhead kick. As the high ball fell into the 6 yard box, the unlikely figure of Pires leapt to meet it, but had timed his run fractionally wrong. The ball bounced out to the marauding Cole, whose cross found Pires again and this time he slotted it home. Newcastle appealed for handball amid the celebrations but the goal stood.

Arsenal should have extended their lead before half-time but instead they found themselves with a precarious lead and only ten men with which to defend it. Parlour had been booked earlier in the game for an elbow to the head of Dabizas and as the half came to a close he brought down Shearer with a sliding tackle. It was a relatively innocuous foul and, in an unusual show of sportsmanship, a number of Newcastle players, among them Shearer, appeared to urge referee Graham Poll to keep his cards in his pocket, but his mind was made up and Parlour walked.

Fifteen minutes into the second half, Newcastle made the most of their numerical advantage by equalising through O'Brien, when the defender headed home at the near post following a corner from substitute Lua-Lua. Then, with 72 minutes on the clock, the referee caused further controversy when he sent off Newcastle's Bellamy for swinging an arm into the face of Cole. It seemed a harsh decision, perhaps motivated by a desire to redress the balance after Parlour's first-half dismissal, but his most contentious ruling was still to come.

As the game entered its final 5 minutes, Arsenal got caught committing men forward and as Newcastle broke midfielder Pires found himself as the home team's last means of defence. A neat ball behind him put Robert through on goal and as he prepared to shoot, Campbell arrived with a last ditch tackle and nicked the ball away for a corner. Except the referee pointed to the spot.

It was an appalling decision, with television replays showing that Campbell got a clean and comprehensive touch on the ball. To compound matters, Shearer stepped up to convert the penalty and Arsenal's disastrous night was completed when Robert finished off a swift Newcastle break by slotting the ball past Taylor. Newcastle had won a match in London at their thirtieth attempt.

The manner of the defeat was too much for Henry and he had to be restrained as he attempted to confront the referee at the final whistle.

He was eventually escorted off the pitch by Metropolitan Police, though rumours that he had been officially cautioned proved to be false.

But it was the first time in his Arsenal career that he had reacted in such a volatile manner. His bad-tempered on-pitch demeanour had become familiar and he certainly wasn't shy about giving referees a piece of his mind, but never before had he gone nuclear in such a way.

Writing in the following day's *Daily Telegraph*, Henry Winter claimed Henry had acquired a reputation among domestic officials that would ensure a hefty suspension:

> English referees have noted his verbal abuse of referees in Europe, notably Manuel Vito Pereira in the Panathinaikos tie, and clearly Poll, in his report, has decided to teach Henry a lesson.

To no-one's surprise, Wenger jumped to the defence of his star striker. 'Players are human beings after all,' he argued, which may have shocked those who had come to assume that Henry was in fact from another planet.

He also received backing from the footballing brotherhood, with teammate Vieira claiming that, 'Thierry is an emotional and passionate person, the kind of guy who does not like injustice. Thierry felt that the referee robbed us of the chance to go top.'

Newcastle midfielder Dyer also invoked a similar defence. 'Thierry Henry was upset, but that just shows how much he cares. People say foreigners are only here for the money but he is passionate and wants to die for the Arsenal shirt.'

Years later, in an interview with *FourFourTwo* magazine, Henry was asked about the incident:

> Some of my teammates came over to pull me away, yes, but only because they thought I was going to lose it. That wasn't the case. When I went over to Poll, there was no one around, so if I had wanted to touch him, I'd have touched him. I just wanted to talk to him face to face [...] I simply asked why he had ruined the game: ruined it for Newcastle and ruined it for us. He wasn't able to provide me with an answer. If you're a man, you can reply. Everybody makes mistakes.

Newcastle's dramatic victory did nothing to temper the perspective of Newcastle manager Bobby Robson. 'You've got to learn how to lose,' he said after the match. 'They should learn how to lose around here.'

As it turned out, they didn't need to. Henry's subsequent three-match suspension only served to motivate Arsenal, who would not lose another league game all season.

19

Arsenal 4 Everton 3
Premier League
11 May 2002

When Her Majesty's finest chaperoned an enraged Henry off the pitch back in December after Arsenal's controversial and demoralising home defeat to Newcastle, few would have imagined that they would not lose another league game all season. Yet when they lined up to face Everton at Highbury for the campaign's curtain call, they were 90 minutes away from that very achievement.

In reality, even a defeat would have been academic. Three days earlier, with Henry absent through injury, Arsenal had wrapped up the League title with a thrilling 1-0 victory at Manchester United, and four days before that the FA Cup with victory over Chelsea at Cardiff's Millennium Stadium to complete the club's second double success in four seasons.

Following that Newcastle loss in December, Arsenal responded with great fortitude, travelling to Liverpool five days later and grinding out a 2-1 victory despite having Van Bronckhorst sent off early in the match. A Henry penalty to open the scoring proved to be his last league goal for a month, but by the start of April he had notched up twenty-two, putting him in contention for the Premier League's Golden Boot award to complement his League and FA Cup winner's medals. Even Champions League elimination at the group stage in March had failed to stifle Arsenal's run.

With Arsenal already champions and Everton safe from relegation, Henry's quest for the Golden Boot was all that prevented the final game of the season being played out as a mere victory parade.

Team: Wright (84), Dixon, Stepanovs, Luzhny, Cole, Parlour (64), Grimandi, Edu, Wiltord (65), Bergkamp, Henry
Subs: Taylor (84), Jeffers (64), Vieira (65)

Despite his impressive goals tally, it would be unfair to say that Henry had singlehandedly inspired Arsenal to the double. Indeed, several other players, most notably Campbell, Ljungberg and Pires, had arguably been equally influential in Arsenal's success. But what Henry had achieved was a consistency of excellence, his flamboyant talents matched by focus, dedication and graft. In just three seasons at Highbury, he had propelled himself into the pantheon of English football's greatest ever strikers.

Henry went into the last game of the season against Everton in a four-man tussle for the Golden Boot, with the Frenchman joined by Newcastle's Shearer, Chelsea's Hasselbaink and Man United's Van Nistelrooy, who were all vying for the coveted award. In a game with nothing at stake for either team, it ensured that at least one player on the pitch wasn't lacking in motivation.

Perhaps unsurprisingly, the relaxed atmosphere of the crowd seemed to filter through to the players, leading to a lack of concentration and a glut of defensive errors in the opening moments of the game. After just 3 minutes, Everton's Stubbs allowed Cole to prod the ball across goal where Bergkamp fired home from 8 yards.

In the 19th minute, it was Arsenal's turn to display some slapstick defending when Stepanovs gifted the ball to Radzinski, who found Carsley, and the midfielder steered an excellent right-footed effort inside the near post. Soon after, Arsenal gifted Everton a second goal when Luzhny allowed Radzinski to turn him near the halfway line and the Canadian sprinted clear of Dixon before slotting a shot past Wright.

The comical defending did not stop there. Just 2 minutes after Everton had taken the lead, Stubbs made his second mistake of the half when he tripped and allowed Bergkamp the chance to slip a pass to Henry who knocked the ball into an open goal. Henry's 23rd goal of the season had been assisted by a player who, it sometimes seemed, was put on this earth to play with him.

Bergkamp had achieved legendary status at Highbury since arriving from Italian club Inter Milan in 1996. Like Henry, he had struggled in Italy and found refuge in the more liberating (and, in truth, more defensively weak) English game. Bergkamp's vision and Henry's pace meant they dovetailed perfectly and although the Dutchman was no longer a permanent fixture in the team, when they were on the pitch together, it was often with devastating effect.

In the 71st minute, Henry combined with another of the club's pass-masters to notch his 24th of the season and put Arsenal in the lead, nudging him ahead of his competitors for the Golden Boot. A diagonal pass from the elegant Brazilian Edu was expertly chested down by Henry on the right of the penalty area and he stroked the ball home.

There was still time for two more goals, first when Jeffers – on as a substitute for Arsenal against his old club – nodded home at the far post from Henry's cross. Then Everton's Watson drifted in from the right and unleashed a left-footed drive past substitute goalkeeper Taylor, who had been brought on to ensure he reached ten appearances for the season, the minimum required to entitle him to a title winner's medal.

The full-time whistle blew and Henry's personal achievement had provided the icing on an already lavish cake. The Highbury pitch was rapidly set up for the presentation ceremony during which captain Tony Adams, who would retire that summer after nineteen years' service, would lift the trophy. Pires, who had emerged as a truly world-class player before suffering a season-ending injury in March that would also rule him out of France's World Cup campaign that summer, held the trophy aloft and his teammates promptly fell to their knees and bowed down to him in comical homage.

After the game, Henry was quick to pay tribute to his captain Adams, as well as another stalwart defender, Dixon, who would also be hanging up his boots that summer.

'They've been the backbone at Arsenal,' said Henry after the game. 'When you have won the title in three decades like they have...'

But Henry was busy making his own history and creating a legacy that would place him in the ranks of Arsenal – and football – legends.

20

France 0 Uruguay 0
World Cup Group Match
6 June 2002

As he prepared for France's World Cup defence as a reigning world champion, European champion, English double winner and Premier League top scorer, Henry was now as decorated as the British Pearly Kings and Queens.

In Henry and the Italian Serie A top scorer Trezeguet, France boasted two of the world's finest strikers, while the old guard at the back had only been shorn of one member, Blanc, to international retirement. With coach Lemerre's squad blessed with such a mix of experience and talent, France went into the tournament as strong favourites to retain their crown.

But the danger of complacency lingers over every sporting team that has experienced such heightened success, and so it was that the football world looked on in shock as their opening game against first-time qualifiers Senegal became the scene of one of the greatest upsets in World Cup history, with the Africans winning 1-0.

No excuse was good enough. Even with their talismanic midfielder Zidane missing through injury and Henry impaired by a knee problem, the holders still should have had more than enough to deal with the Senegalese fledglings. But the nagging truth was that something seemed to have changed in this French side.

One thing was certain: there was no more room for error in France's second group match against Uruguay if they were to avoid the ignominy of becoming the first defending champions to fail to make it to the second round since Brazil in 1966. They had shown they were adept at coping with intense pressure, and with over 600 caps between them the team that lined up against Uruguay had few excuses. It was time to show why they still deserved to be considered the world's greatest national side.

Team: Barthez, Thuram, Leboeuf (16), Desailly, Lizarazu, Vieira, Petit, Wiltord (93+3), Micoud, Henry, Trezeguet (81)
Subs: Candela (16), Cissé (81), Dugarry (90+3)

France started the match like a team looking to make amends, and after just 7 minutes had the ball in the net courtesy of Trezeguet, only for the goal to be ruled out for offside. Soon after, Henry, playing out on the left, was put through on goal but once again the flag went up and France were denied.

With the defending champions pushing for an early goal, a spanner in the works arrived when defender Leboeuf limped off injured and was replaced by Candela who went to right back, with Thuram moving across to centre-half.

The enforced change seemed to knock France off their rhythm and Uruguay sounded a warning when Gilberto broke through and played the ball to Recoba, who forced Barthez into a smart save. But worse was to follow for France with a moment of madness that was as much out of character as it was a hammer blow to France's hopes of staying in the tournament.

Uruguay botched a free kick out on their left by playing it straight to Henry, but as the Frenchman tried to launch a counter attack he mismanaged the ball, allowing it to trickle back into Uruguayan possession. Frustrated by his mistake, Henry launched himself into a dangerous studs-up challenge on Uruguay midfielder Romero, and the referee needed little time to make up his mind, promptly showing him the red card.

It had shades of England's David Beckham in 1998 when he was sent off for a reckless kick out at Argentina's Simeone – an incident that led to him becoming a public hate-figure back home. Henry would avoid quite such a harsh fate, but his lack of self-restraint had certainly dealt a hammer blow to his team's chances of progressing.

Tempers frayed towards the end of the half as the tension started to show on both sides. Gilberto was lucky to stay on the pitch for Uruguay when he caught Vieira and, shortly after half-time, he was deservedly booked.

Micoud went close for France with a free-kick in the 68th minute and, in injury-time, Wiltord had a chance to snatch victory but he delayed his shot and fired over the bar. Then, at the very death, Uruguay could have nicked it when Magallanes' late effort was well saved by Barthez.

The final whistle went and France remained in the tournament by a whisker, needing to beat Denmark by two clear goals in their final group game to make the knockout phase.

With a bandaged-up Zidane making his first appearance back in the side, but Henry suspended, France capitulated against Denmark, losing 2-0. From its wise old heads to its hungry young stars, an inexplicable malaise seemed to have infected the entire France side.

Whether they could return to former glories remained to be seen, but first they would have to face a post-mortem that, once conducted, pointed towards a culture of complacency that had taken hold of the entire French set-up, from junior squad members to high-ranking officials. In short, success had gone to their heads.

Not yet twenty-five and still on an upward career trajectory, there was no question of Henry being a victim of any rebuilding enterprise. Indeed, the majority of the French side were still young enough to compete, if not in the European Championships in two years' time, then certainly the Confederations Cup to be held in France the following summer.

Nonetheless, while Henry dodged becoming the scapegoat for France's collapse (rightly so, given he played his two games nursing an injury) the tournament created an impression among the French public that he had not fulfilled his potential on the international stage, certainly when compared against his evolution at Arsenal.

Henry would have other opportunities to prove them wrong, but the 2002 World Cup became an unwelcome punctuation point in his career. He had already taken on the world and won, but perhaps that was the root of the problem: when you're at the top, the only way is down. Henry, however, would soon rise again.

21

Arsenal 3 Tottenham Hotspur 0
Premier League
16 November 2002

There is no better way to endear yourself to a crowd than to score against your local rivals, and Henry had achieved the feat twice in his three seasons at the club. When Tottenham made the short journey across north London for a league match in November, he was hoping to add to that tally, as well as to a modest return of nine goals in nineteen appearances so far that season for the reigning champions.

After a hugely encouraging start to their title defence, Arsenal had fallen into a mini-slump over the previous month. In mid-October at Everton's Goodison Park, a last-minute wonder goal by a sixteen-year-old Wayne Rooney brought to an end Arsenal's thirty-game unbeaten league run, which stretched all the way back to December 2001. The nature of the defeat seemed to knock Arsenal off their stride and it was followed by home defeats to Auxerre in the Champions League, Blackburn in the league and then another European defeat away to Borussia Dortmund.

Nonetheless, they headed into the Tottenham fixture having won their previous two league games and were just a point behind leaders Liverpool when the game kicked off, with the Merseysiders not due to play until the following day. It was an opportunity to embark on another unbeaten run that could help them retain the League title.

Team: Shaaban, Luzhny, Campbell, Cygan, Cole, Wiltord, Vieira (78), Gilberto, Ljungberg, Henry (75), Bergkamp (26)
Subs: Pires (26), Jeffers (75), Van Bronckhorst (78)

Far from your typical nervy local derby, Arsenal began the game firmly on the front foot and within 4 minutes they had the ball in the net. Cole crossed from the left and Wiltord converted, but the linesman's flag went up for offside.

Spurs were struggling to hold on, and when the goal did eventually arrive in the 13th minute, it was not so much the consequence of Arsenal's pressure as a display of individual brilliance. A Tottenham throw-in deep in Arsenal territory was headed clear to Henry and from well inside his own half he glided forward, leaving an assortment of Tottenham players in his wake. He held off Etherington and, as he approached the edge of the Tottenham box, jinked past Carr and King before driving the ball low into the corner.

Henry celebrated by running back the entire length of the pitch and sliding to his knees just metres in front of the Tottenham fans, his fists clenched by his side and a snarled expression on his face in what would become an iconic image.

One photograph in particular, taken from behind Henry, would become a fans' favourite, and, like the best pieces of art, offers something new every time it is viewed. Amid the inevitable vein-popping fury and obscene hand gestures, one or two spectators stand out as being of a more gentlemanly disposition – notably the chap taking an opportune photograph of the goalscorer and another looking on with a wry, almost reverential smile.

If the Spurs fans could find some tainted comfort in the sheer wonder of what they had just seen, any such sentiments would disappear when, 9 minutes later, the referee sent off Davies for two bookable offences. If the first was deserved, the second, for a fractionally late challenge on Vieira, seemed incredibly harsh. Tottenham hadn't been able to contain Henry with eleven men, so how on earth would they fare with ten?

Spurs somehow managed to get to half-time still only 1-0 down, but almost as soon as the second half began the pattern of the first resumed. Nine minutes in, Arsenal doubled their advantage when Henry turned provider and squared the ball for Ljungberg to score with a simple finish.

With 19 minutes left, Arsenal wrapped up victory when Henry was played through on goal and after Keller saved the initial shot, Pires latched onto the loose ball and passed to Wiltord to fire home from 5 yards.

The comprehensive nature of Arsenal's win over the old enemy would be consigned to the recesses of the mind thanks to Henry's astonishing goal, which, in just 11 seconds (the time between him collecting the ball and scoring), demonstrated the full panoply of his talents. There were many other examples of players running from their own half to score, but few combined such a mix of power, strength, control, technique and coolness. Henry was rapidly revising opinions about what was possible on a football pitch.

22

AS Roma 1 Arsenal 3
Champions League Group Match
27 November 2002

The 2002/03 edition of the Champions League was the last that would feature two group stages before the knockout rounds began. A common complaint among fans was that having to play twelve matches – often against inferior opposition – before reaching the business end of the competition was overkill and so the powers that be decided to ditch it.

But there was nothing dull about the draw for Arsenal's second group stage, which saw them pitted against Roma, Ajax and Valencia. Faced with such stellar opposition, it was clear that they would need to pull out all the stops to beat their previous best in the tournament, when they fell at the quarter-final stage in 2001.

Morale ahead of their opening fixture against Roma in the Italian capital had been affected by a disappointing away league defeat to Southampton four days earlier. As reigning title holders, they had started the season superbly but in the five weeks prior to the Roma match had lost three league games as well as suffering defeats in Europe and the League Cup.

But this was still an Arsenal side more than capable of qualifying from their group and in Henry they had a player who many were tipping to pick up the FIFA World Player of the Year award to be announced less than three weeks later. With his goal against Tottenham at Highbury eleven days earlier, when he ran with the ball from inside his own half, still fresh in the memory, Henry now carried an aura that made it feel like anything was possible.

Team: Shaaban, Luzhny, Campbell, Cygan, Cole, Ljungberg (90), Vieira, Gilberto, Pires (78), Wiltord (84), Henry
Subs: Van Bronckhorst (78), Keown (84), Edu (90)

Arsenal went into the game depleted by injuries, with goalkeeper Seaman joining Bergkamp, Parlour and Kanu on the sidelines against a Roma side that had failed to win any of their three home matches in the first group stage. Ominously for the Italians, Arsenal had already scored impressive victories away at PSV Eindhoven and Auxerre.

Roma showed no sign of nerves in front of their home side and took the lead after just 4 minutes with their first meaningful attack, Cassano slipping his shot past reserve goalkeeper Shaaban.

But Roma fans had barely finished celebrating when Arsenal hit back. Gilberto showed neat footwork before playing a deft pass that split the Roma defence and found Henry, who broke into the box on the left before stroking the ball into the far corner. It was a textbook Henry goal, replicated endless times throughout his career, where he collected the ball in the inside left position before opening out his body and placing a side-footed shot that every goalkeeper must have anticipated yet few could do anything about.

The goal calmed Arsenal nerves and Arsenal started passing the ball around with great confidence. They continued to dictate the pace after the interval and with 20 minutes left Henry struck again. Panucci was unable to clear Luzhny's cross from the right and Henry pounced on the loose ball before firing through the legs of Antonioli from close range.

The goal took the wind out of Roma and they never recovered. Just 5 minutes after going in front, Arsenal earned a free kick 25 yards from goal. Henry stepped up and floated a delicious curling effort into the top corner. His first ever European hat trick had virtually assured Arsenal of a crucial victory.

Back in the late 1990s, when Henry drew attention with a string of eye-catching European performances, it was in the relatively dim spotlight that came with playing for Monaco. But now he was competing for a club that had genuine aspirations of winning the trophy and joining the European elite. His already soaring reputation had just been raised several more notches.

23

Manchester City 1 Arsenal 5
Premier League
26 February 2003

With seven months of the season gone, Arsenal seemed firmly on course for retaining the League title for the first time since 1934 (a golden era in the club's history in which they won the league five times in eight years). They were even still in the running for the treble, having progressed to the quarter-finals of the FA Cup and remaining in the running to qualify out of their Champions League group – though they were making hard work of the latter.

However, it was not just their results that had impressed, but the manner in which they were achieved. Some were even questioning whether this was the greatest football the English game had ever seen.

Arsenal were now known the world over for their fast, fluid style of play that would often result in goals of such aesthetic beauty that they would not look out of place as performance art. As much as fans are loath to use the word, there was no denying that Arsène Wenger had created a 'brand' of football that had revamped the club's image.

At the fulcrum of their regular masterclasses was Henry, who had already notched twenty-four goals for the season. Back in November, he had lit up the Champions League with a hat-trick in Arsenal's group match at Italian club Roma and then immediately after Christmas he burst out of the blocks, scoring eight goals in just five matches.

By the time Arsenal's away league match with Manchester City came around, they were unbeaten in their last fifteen games. With title rivals Manchester United dropping points in their away fixture at Bolton in an earlier kick-off, Arsenal stood to go five points clear if they could secure three points at Man City.

Team: Taylor, Lauren, Keown, Campbell, Van Bronckhorst, Pires (74), Gilberto, Vieira, Wiltord (74), Bergkamp (64), Henry
Subs: Parlour (64), Edu (74), Jeffers (74)

The main team news for Arsenal was the selection of Taylor in goal, in for the injured Seaman, but if the reserve 'keeper was hoping to make an impression, he had been dealt the worst possible game to try as he remained a virtual bystander for almost the entire match.

Arsenal dominated the early stages and after just 4 minutes took the lead after Bergkamp ghosted past the hosts' defence and slotted the ball home. Eight minutes later, Arsenal doubled their lead when Dunne played a loose ball out of City's defence, which was intercepted by Henry in his favourite inside-left position. He drove at the City defence, skipping around Dunne with ease and cutting the ball back from the by-line for Pires to shoot left-footed past City goalkeeper Nash.

Man City were shell-shocked, but for Arsenal it seemed like just another day at the office. Three minutes later they scored a third goal of such simple beauty that it took the breath away. Keown played a long ball from defence that drifted over the head of Dunne and into the path of Henry who had pulled away to the left of the penalty box. An ordinary player would have focused all his efforts on controlling a difficult pass before weighing up his options, but this was Henry. He brought the ball down with the laces of his right foot and in almost the same movement launched a powerful but controlled left-footed shot which nestled in the far corner.

After 19 minutes, with Arsenal's defence barely having touched the ball, Campbell decided to join in the fun and after Henry launched a corner (by this point in his Arsenal career he had assumed all set piece responsibilities, to the annoyance of those who thought a 6-foot striker would be better off on the end of crosses) into the box the England centre-back rose and headed powerfully beyond Nash for Arsenal's fourth.

It had been a mind-blowing spell of probing build-up play and calculated finishing from Arsenal and represented perhaps the apex of a season in which they had frequently taken football to new heights.

Understandably, Arsenal took their foot off the gas for the remainder of the half and restricted themselves to just a solitary goal after the break, with captain Patrick Vieira adding his name to the score-sheet. Former Arsenal striker Anelka, who had failed to fulfil his talent and arrived in Manchester via disappointing spells at Real Madrid, Paris St Germain and Liverpool, scored a late consolation against his old club but it took none of the gloss off of what had been a scintillating display of attacking football.

But more than that, the result underlined Arsenal's superiority in the Premiership, putting them in pole position to preserve their League title with a quarter of the season to go.

'You look at yourself and ask if it is really happening,' said the City defender Steve Howey after the match,

> When they play like that you just can't stop them. It's awful. There are players coming at you from every direction. You stop Henry and there's Pires. Or Bergkamp. Or Wiltord. You can stop one or two but you can't stop them all [...] I think we have seen today that Arsenal have proved they are the best team in the Premiership. Emphatically. As a professional you just want a shred of pride back. You don't want it to be a farce but 4-0 down after 19 minutes is farcical by anyone's standards.

Kevin Keegan, the City manager, went even further, predicting that Arsenal would triumph in Europe too. 'Arsenal, in my opinion, will win the Champions League,' he said with conviction. 'They're on a different planet.'

Arsenal 1 Southampton 0
FA Cup Final
17 May 2003

It was the third consecutive year the FA Cup final was to be played at the Millennium Stadium in Cardiff due to the ongoing reconstruction of Wembley Stadium, and Arsenal already had fond memories of the interim venue following their victory over Chelsea in the previous year's showpiece.

There had been, however, little to reminiscence about over the past few months that would offer happiness to anyone connected with Arsenal, save for their progress to the Cup final. Having entered the last third of the season looking odds on to retain the League title, they had surrendered their position of strength to Manchester United, as well as exiting the Champions League at the group stage. Given that not long ago some had been tipping them for the treble, that they were now facing the prospect of a comparatively humble FA Cup victory was hard to take.

Arsenal had certainly gone off the boil over the previous few months, but they would still go into the final as firm favourites. Henry, who was still seeking the first competitive Cup final goal of his career, remained Arsenal's main threat and had notched seven goals in his last seven games, including two for France in a friendly versus Egypt. He had also enhanced his assists record, which stood at a hugely impressive twenty-three for the season, and it was an aspect of his game he was keen to emphasise.

Speaking ahead of the game, he said,

I'm not only a goalscorer. Sometimes people put me in the same league as [Michael] Owen or Van Nistelrooy but I'm not at all like this type [...] the one thing I was pleased with this season was the goals I gave. I think it's pretty rare to see a striker with that amount of assists.

Henry, who collected the PFA Player of the Year award in the week leading up to the Cardiff final, also denied that victory would be undermined by their disappointments in the league:

> There is no anti-climax. At the end you have to give credit to Manchester United. They did well to come back and we didn't do enough to keep our lead. But life goes on. We have had worse seasons. We are still in the FA Cup and we were competing for the title. Maybe everyone was expecting us to retain the title but we didn't. Now we must come back even stronger.

What better way to start than to win the FA Cup and in doing so becoming the first team to retain the trophy since Tottenham Hotspur in 1982? This was certainly no consolation prize.

But one other spectre lingered over the occasion, and that was Henry's dwindling contract, which was now down to its final two years. Arsenal were due to move into their new stadium at Ashburton Grove in three years' time and the prospect of them doing so without their leading light was unthinkable. But with many fans concerned that the club would have to divert funds towards serving the stadium debt rather than investing it on the pitch, it seemed fair to wonder whether Henry – and indeed Arsenal's other star players – would want to spend their peak years at a club lacking the money to compete.

Henry gave an interview in the days before the final that did little to quell concerns that his future lay elsewhere. 'I'm a loyal guy,' he said,

> Whatever happens I will respect it. Because, as I always say, the team, the fans, the club, they gave me a hand when I left Juventus and I was a bit down. I can never forget that. All I can do is my best on the pitch. Listen to me, right now my mind is focused on Arsenal and there is nothing else. But I can't put myself where I'll be in five or six years' time. For us players all these kind of questions are difficult because we don't know exactly what's going on. I don't like to talk about things I don't control. But I understand what you're saying, that if a player sees that things don't change, he might leave.

Team: Seaman, Lauren, Luzhny, Keown, Cole, Ljungberg, Parlour, Gilberto, Pires, Henry, Bergkamp (77)
Subs: Wiltord (77)

The game was lent an incongruous atmosphere as the first Cup final to be played indoors, with the high-tech Millennium Stadium roof closed due to bad weather. There was also a moment of mild awkwardness during the traditional pre-match meet-and-greet with the Football Association's chief guest of honour, Sir Bobby Robson, who the previous season had been critical of Henry after the Frenchman had reacted badly to Arsenal's home defeat against Robson's Newcastle. Henry's embarrassed laughter as he shook the former England boss's hand suggested that at least one of them hadn't forgotten the incident.

One player for whom the game meant more than most was Arsenal goalkeeper Seaman, who was making his last appearance for the club. The semi-final versus Sheffield United marked his 1,000th appearance in senior football and he was now hoping to bow out with a trophy. In the absence of the injured Vieira (like Henry, the subject of growing speculation linking him with a summer move), Seaman was named captain for the final.

The other significant team news for Arsenal was the loss of Campbell who was suspended following his red card at Highbury against Manchester United a month earlier. His replacement was the Ukranian Luzhny.

Within minutes Arsenal should have taken the lead when Henry evaded a shirt-tug from defender Lundekvam and brought a one-handed save from Niemi at the near post. Had Henry gone to ground, Arsenal would almost certainly have been handed a penalty and a one-man advantage, as Lundekvam would surely have been sent off for a professional foul.

After the game, Lundekvam would acknowledge Henry's fair play (though ironically the Frenchman was later booked for diving in a separate incident).

> By staying on his feet he did me a big favour. If he had gone down I would have been in trouble. He's a very honest player and during one of those quiet moments that you get in the course of a game I thanked him.

But in the early stages, quiet moments were few and far between for the Southampton defence and it was Henry at the centre of everything. In the 7th minute, he forced another save from Niemi and, when the goalkeeper failed to hold the ball, Baird had to make a goal-line clearance after Bergkamp followed up with a shot from a narrow angle. Henry broke free again 3 minutes later, beating Lundekvam with ease, before shooting weakly.

Midway through the half, Southampton eventually created a chance of their own when Baird forced the first save out of Seaman with a dipping long-range drive. But Arsenal responded by sweeping forward to break the deadlock 7 minutes before the interval. Henry played in Bergkamp, and when Ljungberg's shot was blocked, the rebound fell invitingly for Pires to score from 8 yards.

Seven minutes into the second half, Arsenal spurned a glorious opportunity to double their advantage when Ljungberg could only find the side-netting after Niemi parried Bergkamp's shot into his path. It was then only a fingertip intervention from Niemi that stopped Henry 4 minutes later as he attempted a curling finish.

It turned out to be the goalkeeper's last contribution as he pulled up in agony after 64 minutes clutching his calf after taking a goal-kick and was stretchered off, to be replaced by substitute 'keeper Jones.

At the other end, Seaman was enjoying a rather inconspicuous end to his Arsenal career, but the final 10 minutes saw him called into action on several occasions. The best chance came when Ormerod's powerful drive seemed destined for the top corner until Seaman flung out a hand to divert his shot to safety.

In the final minutes Arsenal engaged in some dubious time-wasting, persistently taking the ball into the corner, with the main culprit being Henry. It seemed out of character for a player who professed to love entertaining. But he had been the game's stand-out performer, a constant menace to Southampton and a deserved recipient of the Man of the Match award. He had earned the right to kill some seconds and help see out the game.

After the match, Southampton manager Gordon Strachan applauded Henry's performance, describing his centre backs as 'like two dead bodies in the dressing room. They have played against the world's best striker and I think it has aged each of them four years.'

Henry still didn't have a Cup final goal to his name, but no-one was in any doubt of the enormity of his contribution to a piece of silverware that represented a silver lining to Arsenal's season.

25

Cameroon 0 France 1
Confederations Cup Final
29 June 2003

The trauma of South Korea and Japan a year earlier, where Henry was a peripheral figure in France's ignominious abdication of their World Cup crown, was now a distant memory. Thirty-two goals and twenty-four assists across the 2002/03 season with Arsenal was incontrovertible proof that Henry was not only back in form, but operating at the very peak of his powers.

His English contemporaries seemed to agree, with both the Professional Footballers' Association and Football Writers' Association voting Henry their player of the year for 2003. England was now his spiritual home and Highbury, as he would later describe it, was his garden.

But back in his birthplace, Henry had not yet won over the French public. It was true that he had often failed to replicate his scintillating club performances for his country, but there were mitigating factors that accounted for this. After all, at the 1998 World Cup, he had arguably been promoted to the team ahead of schedule and despite finishing as France's top scorer, it was clear to most that he was still an unrefined talent. Then in 2002, following the unalloyed success of France's Euro 2000 campaign in which Henry was excellent throughout, he struggled with injury and was eventually forced out of their final match against Denmark which lead to their elimination.

The 2003 Confederations Cup, to be hosted by France, represented a quick opportunity for redemption for Henry and several other players who retained their places in the squad chosen by new coach Jacques Santini. One key absentee, however, was Zidane who it was decided would be rested.

France negotiated their way through the tournament with impressive ease, though it would be fair to say that a group comprising Columbia, Japan and New Zealand hardly represented top notch opposition. But the form of Henry in particular had stood out, and by the time they despatched Turkey at the semi-final stage, he had earned three Man of the Match awards and scored four goals into the bargain.

But it was the other semi-final, between Cameroon and Columbia, for which the tournament would forever be remembered due to a tragedy that rendered footballing matters irrelevant. In the 72nd minute, twenty-eight-year-old Cameroon midfielder Marc-Vivien Foe collapsed to the ground unchallenged. He was treated on the pitch before being stretchered off to receive further treatment, including mouth-to-mouth resuscitation and extra oxygen, but died in the stadium's medical centre. The cause of his death was heart failure, possibly due to a pre-existing but undiagnosed condition.

The natural reaction of everyone involved in the competition was that the final should not be played, and this seemed to be the likely outcome until Foe's wife intervened and insisted that the game go ahead as a tribute to her husband.

Despite strong reservations in both camps, and in circumstances no footballer would ever wish to face, it was decided that the game would be played. France and Cameroon would contest the final to honour their fallen colleague.

Team: Barthez, Sagnol (76), Desailly, Gallas, Lizarazu, Giuly, Pedretti, Dacourt (90), Wiltord (65), Cisse, Henry
Subs: Pires (65), Thuram (76), Kapo (90)

As a mark of respect for the passing of Marc-Vivien Foe, the captain of each team – Song of Cameroon and France's Desailly – held a picture of the deceased midfielder as they led their sides out at the Stade de France in Paris.

A minute's silence was then observed as players from both sides intermingled and linked arms in the centre circle, with each Cameroon player wearing Foe's No. 17 on their warm-up shirt, with his name written on the back.

Understandably, the match was slow in building up momentum before Henry created the first chance in the 22nd minute, crossing for Cissé who headed wide, to give the contest some impetus.

Cameroon immediately exerted a spell of pressure on the French goal with Idrissou and Djemba Djemba both going close, but France were soon back on the front-foot, with Henry their main threat.

Despite concerted French pressure, Cameroon held on until half-time and the same tone continued into the second period with the African side persistently rebuffing France's efforts to make a breakthrough.

An ambitious Henry half-volley went close for France but Cameroon nearly took a shock lead when substitute Eto'o found himself free at the far post only to shoot wide.

The game went into extra-time with both teams aware that the 'Golden Goal' rule was in play, meaning that a single mistake or moment of magic from either side could win or lose the trophy.

Seven minutes in, France secured victory and it was Henry who proved the match winner, latching onto a pass over the top of the defence and flicking an improvised shot beyond the Cameroon goalkeeper from the edge of the 6 yard box. Henry hurdled the advertising boards and went to the crowd in celebration. It was his first ever career goal in a competitive final, and in spite of the emotional backdrop to the occasion, few would have denied him the chance to savour the moment.

Henry's goal and all-round performance in the final completed a superb tournament that saw him furnished with four Man of the Match awards, the Golden Ball (after being voted the competition's outstanding player) and the Golden Shoe (for finishing top scorer).

Euro 2000 notwithstanding, Henry's international statistics were now beyond dispute. As much as the 2003 Confederations Cup would rightly come to be defined by Cameroon's tragic loss, it also undeniably represented a crossroad in the perception of Henry among his countryfolk, who finally believed him worthy of the kind of adoration he received so frequently in his 'garden' at Highbury.

26

Inter Milan 1 Arsenal 5
Champions League Group Match
25 November 2003

A disastrous start to Arsenal's Champions League campaign meant that Arsenal travelled to Milan with their hopes of progressing in the competition firmly in the balance. A single point from their opening three group games – including a comprehensive 3-0 defeat at home to Inter Milan – followed by a last gasp victory against Dynamo Kiev at Highbury, meant that they faced one of the powerhouses of European football needing at least a draw to avoid crashing out of Europe at the first hurdle.

Their European form had been in stark contrast to their performances in the league, which had seen them unbeaten since the start of the season. The Inter Milan away fixture followed a run of seven league wins in eight and some of the football they were playing was sublime.

But they had not yet cracked Europe and no-one quite knew why. After all, they had a multi-national team of established internationals and a manager whose knowledge of the European game was second to none. Why could their domestic form not be transferred to the European stage?

Though he had not scored in Arsenal's first four European group games, no one was pointing the finger at Henry. His sensational performances in the league combined with his star role in France's summer Confederations Cup success had, for the time being, insulated him from criticism. Three days before the Inter Milan game, Birmingham manager Steve Bruce hailed Henry the best player in the world.

That declaration followed Arsenal's 3-0 defeat of Birmingham, in which Henry didn't score, but provided the vital pass for each goal. After the game, Wenger focussed on Henry's ability to create as well as score, saying, 'I like it very much when a striker opts to give the final ball to another player to finish, especially when he has not already scored himself.'

The Inter Milan game would see the convergence of both of these talents in the most dramatic and unlikely fashion, as Henry once again took football to new levels of improbability.

Team: Lehmann, Toure, Cygan, Campbell, Cole, Parlour, Edu, Ljungberg, Pires, Kanu (73), Henry (89)
Subs: Gilberto (73), Aliadiere (89)

If Arsenal didn't already have an unenviable task on their hands then their prospects were made even sterner by the absence of some key personnel in Milan, notably Lauren, Keown, Vieira and Wiltord.

Nonetheless, they made a sprightly start in Milan, knocking the ball around with great confidence though and approaching midway through the first half, Kanu picked up a throw-in 30 yards out, spun sharply, and shot narrowly wide. It seemed to give Arsenal the belief they needed and 4 minutes later they took the lead.

Henry found Cole in the penalty box, but without an angle to shoot he returned the pass first time back to Henry, who was lurking on the edge of the box. It was weighted perfectly for Henry to shoot first time and his right-footed effort nestled in the bottom corner.

Their lead lasted just 8 minutes. Vieiri shot from outside the box and the ball spun wickedly off Campbell's boot and Lehmann could only tip the ball onto the bar before watching helplessly as it bounced into the net.

The final 10 minutes of the half were end-to-end stuff, with both sides forging chances. Having gone into the game in hope rather than expectation, there was now genuine belief within the Arsenal camp that they could eek something out of this game and avert European elimination – if only as a temporary reprieve.

Their confidence would grow even greater just 3 minutes after the restart. Henry collected the ball on the left, and as three Inter players were drawn towards him, Ljungberg made a run into the box. Henry delayed the pass and for a moment it seemed the chance had gone, but no-one had picked up Ljungberg's run, allowing Henry to pick out his Swedish teammate who controlled and shot past Toldo.

The game had to wait another half an hour for another meaningful moment, but when it arrived it was something magical. An Inter Milan corner was cleared by Arsenal and the bouncing ball found Henry deep inside his own half. With Inter having committed all but one player forward, a counter-attack was on, and against Henry of all players, this was pure suicide.

Zanetti was a supreme footballer but faced with Henry's pace it would have been a mismatch. Yet, curiously, Henry chose not to put his main asset into full effect. Perhaps tired or feeling a slight injury, after an initial 20-yard burst he appeared to almost slow down and allow Zanetti to catch him up. As Henry reached the edge of the box, he held the ball up until support arrived in the shape of Pires. The pass was on, and yet Henry again shunned the obvious choice and held onto the ball. By now three defenders were back, and it was the cue for Henry to make his move. He shifted the ball outside of Zanetti again and slammed an immaculate left-footed shot beyond Toldo and into the far corner.

With 5 minutes left, a crucial victory was now in sight but Arsenal were not finished yet. In the final moments, goals from Edu and Pires, including another assist for Henry, produced the kind of scoreline that prompted you to rub your eyes and look again. It was a result that nobody connected with Arsenal could have even dreamed of and Arsenal would go on to qualify for the knockout stages with victory over Lokomotiv Moscow three weeks later.

'I am very proud of the players and the spirit they showed,' said Arsène Wenger after the game. 'Our character came out. We were persistent and we took our chances.'

That so many of these chances were either created or converted by Henry demonstrated perhaps as much as any game in his career his all-encompassing talents. Had there ever before been a player who could both create *and* convert with such proficiency?

27

Arsenal 4 Liverpool 2
Premier League
9 April 2004

They say that a week is a long time in politics, but the seven days that preceded Arsenal's home match with Liverpool on Good Friday must have felt like a lifetime. The Gunners had entered the previous weekend still in with a shout of emulating Manchester United's treble success of 1999, sitting four points clear of Chelsea at the top of the table and facing two crucial cup games – against Man United in the FA Cup and then a Champions League second leg with title rivals Chelsea over the following four days.

Another truism – that confidence is fragile in sport – perhaps applied to Arsenal more than most other clubs. So finely tuned was Arsenal's football philosophy under Wenger and so reliant was it on fast, fluid passing that even the smallest setback could send their entire modus operandi into meltdown. Their vulnerability would contribute to four days that left their treble hopes in tatters.

First they were despatched from the FA Cup, losing 1-0 to Man United, and then in midweek they were knocked out of the Champions League after a 2-1 defeat to Chelsea at Highbury, putting the west Londoners through 3-2 on aggregate. Given how hard they had battled to stay in the competition, the Champions League exit in particular was a bitter pill to swallow.

Having been basking in the glow of a season that promised so much, Arsenal were suddenly in danger of winning nothing. Unbeaten in the league all season, they had been going into games believing they couldn't lose. Now they looked like they had forgotten how to win. Could they find the resources to at least put their title charge back on track?

Team: Lehmann, Lauren, Campbell, Toure, Cole, Ljungberg (89), Vieira, Gilberto, Pires (72), Bergkamp, Henry
Subs: Edu (72), Keown (89)

To a neutral observer, Arsenal appeared in good shape going into the game, with victory standing to put them seven points ahead of Chelsea at the top of the table with just six games to play. But the past week's cup defeats had taken a significant psychological toll and to make matters worse, Henry was carrying a back injury, though he was named in the starting line-up.

Unsurprisingly, Arsenal started the match in tentative fashion and before long Liverpool were in control. After just 5 minutes the away side took the lead when a third Liverpool corner in a row was met by Gerrard whose header was diverted into the net by Hyypia.

Despite Arsenal's lofty league position, no-one in the ground was surprised. They looked utterly devoid of ideas and shorn of all belief, and soon after the opening goal, only a smart intervention from Campbell stopped Owen making it two.

At this point, it was hard to conceive of how they could get back into the game, but after 31 minutes they scored a goal that reminded onlookers of what this side were capable of. Pires picked up a loose ball and saw Henry peeling away from the Liverpool defence. The high ball from Pires was perfect but Henry still had plenty to do. Killing the ball instantly with his right foot, he steadied himself and slotted it with his left under Dudek and into the far corner of the net.

The goal settled Arsenal's nerves, but only momentarily, and their frailties were exposed once again 3 minutes before the interval when Gerrard's slide rule pass found Owen who finished neatly. Arsenal went into the break in real trouble, their mental fragility exposed by their recent travails.

If ever a team needed to show their mettle then this was it. Four minutes into the second half, Henry cut inside and fizzed the ball into the feet of Ljungberg on the edge of the box. He played a first time pass over the Liverpool defence and found Pires, who held off the challenge of Carragher and scuffed a left-footed shot beyond Dudek to level the score.

Just 60 seconds after their equaliser came the latest addition to the Henry oeuvre. The Frenchman had dropped back into midfield and allowed the play to develop in front of him, almost as if he were seeking a better vantage point from which to assess what he would do next. After a Liverpool clearance, Gilberto tapped the ball to Henry some 40 yards from goal. He ran past Redknapp as if he wasn't there and advanced towards the Liverpool box. Faced with a wall of defenders, there seemed no way through, but as he drew two of them out, he bamboozled them both by jinking left. Finding himself with only Dudek to beat, he opened out his body and sidefooted powerfully across the keeper and into the net.

With 12 minutes left, Henry completed his hat-trick, taking advantage of slack marking to bundle home Bergkamp's through ball. Arsenal had reinforced their position of strength at the top of the table and put to bed the lingering memories of the previous week's disappointments.

As for Henry, rarely had a player grabbed a game by the scruff of its neck in such a way, recalling other great virtuoso performances such as that by Maradona at the 1986 World Cup and David Beckham against Greece in England's crucial 2002 World Cup qualifier. For Henry to be talked of in the same breath as such luminaries of the game was entirely justified. He had joined the ranks of the very best.

28

Arsenal 5 Leeds United 0
Premier League
16 April 2004

The 100th ever league meeting between Arsenal and Leeds was significant for wildly contrasting reasons for both clubs. A win for Arsenal would see them surge ten points clear with just five games to play, whereas Leeds were staring down the barrel at the other end of the table.

To make matters worse for the Yorkshire club, in two previous meetings that season at Elland Road, including an FA Cup tie, Arsenal had on both occasions routed them 4-1. Henry in particular had run them ragged, scoring three over the two games. Put simply, Leeds were sick of the sight of Arsenal, although they were not the only ones. Indeed, Arsenal were now unbeaten in their last thirty-four league games and with just five fixtures left there was genuine talk about whether they could go the entire campaign without defeat.

With Henry's match-winning performance a week earlier against Liverpool still fresh in the memory, his hat-trick putting him on thirty-three goals for the season, it felt as if anything was possible.

Team: Lehmann, Lauren, Campbell, Toure, Clichy, Pires (72), Gilberto (69), Vieira, Wiltord, Henry, Bergkamp (72)
Subs: Edu (69) Reyes (72) Parlour (72)

Arsenal fielded close to their full strength side, with only the young French left-back Clichy deputising for Cole. On the bench was Arsenal's January transfer window signing from Seville, the twenty-year-old Spaniard Reyes, considered one of Europe's most gifted youngsters. He had already caught the eye at Highbury during his intermittent appearances so far, most notably in an FA Cup tie at home to Chelsea in which he scored two goals in

5 minutes to give Arsenal victory, including a superb long range drive into the top corner.

After Reyes' winning goal, television commentator John Motson described Henry as the 'King of Highbury' before adding in reference to the match-winner that 'there's a new Prince now'. It was not evident at the time, but question marks would soon arise over their compatibility on the pitch.

In the meantime, all eyes were on Arsenal's seemingly inexorable march to the title. After just 6 minutes, they took the lead when a perfectly weighted Bergkamp through ball was curled around goalkeeper Robinson by Pires. Midway through the half, they extended their lead when Gilberto knocked the ball forward into space and Leeds' abysmal effort at an offside trap left Henry through on goal, who coolly slotted in number two. It was the start of a memorable night's work for the Frenchman.

Victory was all but confirmed after 36 minutes when Bergkamp played a one-two on the edge of the box, and when he tried to dink the ball beyond Duberry the Leeds defender raised his hand to the ball and gave away a penalty.

In contrast with the dazzling variety of his goals, Henry's penalties tended by comparison to be fairly orthodox. But on this occasion, he stepped up and chipped the ball straight down the middle in a style known to football's cognoscenti as a 'Panenka', named after Czech player Antonín Panenka, who scored the winning penalty in the final of the 1976 European Championship against Germany with just such an audacious effort.

Five minutes after the interval, Henry had his second hat-trick in the space of eight days. Set up by Gilberto again, Henry took one touch before sliding the ball past Robinson for another landmark goal.

Incredibly, he wasn't finished there. With 23 minutes left on the clock, Pires collected the ball in a central position with his back to goal and laid it off for Henry, who in the blink of an eye dissected virtually the entire Leeds midfield and defence. Marauding into the Leeds penalty box, he lost balance just as he was about to shoot, but as he fell he had the guile to divert the ball into the net for his fourth goal of the game.

'I've seen most things in this league in the last 25 years ... I've not seen anything like him,' gushed Sky TV co-commentator Andy Gary. It was a view shared increasingly across football. Had there ever been a striker quite like Henry?

His four-goal extravaganza also propelled him up the list of Arsenal's all time record scorers, pushing him into third place after surpassing John Radford's figure of 149.

'It's difficult to find each time new words for Thierry,' Arsène Wenger said after the game.

Rather than talking about him, it's better watching him. When the team is on the same wavelength, with his power and pace and skills, it's a joy to watch. We have many players who can put him through [...] His finishing gets better and I think in recent games he's come back to a more central position again. For a while he went systematically out wide left. With a more central position he's more dangerous.

As well as putting Arsenal in a virtually unassailable position at the top of the table, the victory over Leeds also opened up a delicious prospect that had Arsenal fans licking their lips in devilish anticipation. Next up was Tottenham at White Hart Lane the following weekend, and if Chelsea and Man United both contrived to lose their next respective games, Arsenal could secure the title at the ground of their hated rivals.

29

Tottenham Hotspur 2 Arsenal 2
Premier League
25 April 2004

Thirty-three years had passed since Arsenal visited Tottenham knowing that victory would give them the League title. On that Monday evening in May 1971, striker Ray Kennedy popped up to head the winner for manager Bertie Mee's side, giving Arsenal fans bragging rights over their local rivals that they would dine out on for decades to come.

Fast forward to 25 April 2004 and Arsenal (containing, lest we forget, their neighbours' former captain Sol Campbell) stood to repeat the feat that, if achieved, meant they would have won the league at Tottenham's stadium the same amount of times that Tottenham had won it in their entire history. It was just one of many galling statistics that Spurs fans would have rammed down their throats unless they could do something that no other club that season had managed to do: beat Arsenal in the league.

No player had done more than Henry to put Arsenal in such a position. With thirty-eight goals to his name, he was enjoying his most prolific season for the club and was in line to win not only his second title winner's medal but a litany of personal prizes including both the European and Premier League Golden Boots, the PFA Player's Player of the Year award and the Football Writers' Footballer of the Year award (the latter two for the second year running). If that wasn't enough, he had finished runner-up in both the 2003 FIFA World Player of the Year (to Zinedine Zidane) and Balon d'Or (to Pavel Nedved) awards handed out back in December.

After those latter awards, Arsène Wenger expressed his belief that Henry deserved to be recognised among the elite. 'Although Thierry hasn't won the award, being voted the second best player in the world is fantastic recognition from the world's football coaches,' he said. 'The achievement was to be in the top three. After that it is subjective between Thierry, Zidane or Ronaldo. For me, there is nothing between them.'

If Henry felt a flicker of disappointment to have missed out on the prestigious FIFA and Balon d'Or prizes, then what better way to soften the blow than to wrap up the League title at the ground of the old enemy (again) and with it etch his name even deeper into Arsenal folklore.

His chances of doing just that were made real ahead of kick-off, when Arsenal's closest challenges Chelsea went down 2-1 at Newcastle, meaning that even a draw at White Hart Lane would hand Arsenal the title.

Team: Lehmann, Lauren, Campbell, Toure, Cole, Parlour (67), Vieira, Gilberto, Pires, Henry, Bergkamp (80)
Subs: Edu (67), Reyes (80)

Arsenal were unbeaten in the last eight north London derbies and with Tottenham lingering at the bottom end of the table just above the relegation zone, there was rarely a time in the clubs' modern histories that the gulf between them had been so large.

That gulf in quality was evident within 3 minutes as Arsenal took the lead with a breathtaking goal that epitomised why this side was so special. A Tottenham corner was headed back to the edge of the box and collected by Henry who moved rapidly upfield, evading one challenge and powering along the left wing. As he crossed the halfway line, he looked up and saw Bergkamp making a run behind Tottenham's fullback. Henry slid a pass into the space and Bergkamp played a first-time ball across the box for a stretching Vieira to sidefoot into the corner of the net.

Twelve seconds was all that was needed between Henry receiving the ball and Vieira slotting home, just one second more than Henry's unforgettable goal against the same opposition at Highbury a couple of years earlier when he similarly ran from inside his own half.

If their first goal demonstrated Arsenal's counter-attacking prowess, then their second, after 35 minutes, was a masterclass in possession football. A ten-pass move saw Spurs chasing shadows before the ball arrived at the feet of Bergkamp who had come deep. He turned and played an instant pass inside Tottenham's right back for Vieira who had moved out to the left. As the defender slid in, Vieira cut the ball back for Pires, who caressed a first time shot beyond the Tottenham goalkeeper and into the far corner.

Tottenham increased their tempo after the interval and in the 62nd minute pulled a goal back when Brown rolled a pass for Redknapp to score from 20 yards with a first-time finish.

Still with a two-goal buffer to win the League, Arsenal refused to panic and as the game reached its final moments it was nearly time for the celebrations to begin in earnest. But from a corner in stoppage time, their irascible German goalkeeper Lehmann reacted to being impeded by Keane by pushing the Irishman and, after a consultation with his linesman, the referee pointed to the spot. Keane stepped up and scored an equaliser that sent the crowd wild. It seemed an eye-raising display of cognitive dissonance given that, in just a few seconds time, they would be watching their rivals celebrate winning the League in front of their very eyes.

As it turned out, many Spurs fans around the stadium were unaware that a point would hand Arsenal the title, which may explain their excessive reaction to the equaliser. But when the final whistle went, they soon realised the painful truth.

It would take a few minutes for the elation to come to the surface for Arsenal. Henry, in particular, seemed put out by Spurs' pyrrhic celebrations, wagging his finger at Redknapp, while Lauren remonstrated with the officials over the penalty decision. In a later interview, Henry explained his incredulity:

> I saw [Mauricio] Taricco celebrate so much that he injured himself. I said to him, 'you do realise we only needed a point and now we are celebrating the title on your ground?'

In truth, the fact that Arsenal had given away a two-goal lead did momentarily take the gloss off of what should have been an untarnished occasion of unrestrained joy. But Arsenal weren't going to let the relative triviality of the result ruin their fun.

Minutes after the final whistle, Henry led the cavalcade towards the corner of the ground containing Arsenal's jubilant fans, pulling off his shirt and swinging it around above his head as he ran towards them. For the next half an hour, the Arsenal squad danced and jigged in that corner. One fan chucked an inflatable Premiership trophy onto the pitch, and in lieu of the real thing, Ashley Cole ran and planted it in the centre circle. By this point almost every Spurs fan (save for a handful of masochists) had wisely left the stadium.

Even Arsène Wenger came out to join his players as they milked the moment. He was now the first ever manager of the club to win three League championships and was also now on the brink of becoming the first to guide the club to an unbeaten league season. With four games to go, immortality beckoned, but glory was already theirs.

30

Arsenal 2 Leicester City 1
Premier League
15 May 2004

It's not impossible as AC Milan once did it but I can't see why it's so shocking to say it. Do you think Manchester United, Liverpool or Chelsea don't dream that as well? They're exactly the same. They just don't say it because they're scared to look ridiculous, but nobody is ridiculous in this job as we know anything can happen.

These were the words of Arsène Wenger, spoken in September 2002, and they were met with unbridled derision. Fans and pundits alike lined up to mock his stated belief that Arsenal could go unbeaten for a whole season. One enterprising character even produced T-shirts comparing him to the hapless Iraqi Defence Minister Mohammed Saeed al-Sahhaf, dubbed 'Comical Ali' for maintaining in spite of all evidence to the contrary that his nation was standing firm during the 2003 western military intervention in Iraq.

But here we were twenty months later and Arsenal had indeed stood firm for the preceding thirty-seven league matches – and now there was only one more left to play. With the League title wrapped up four games earlier at Tottenham, their one remaining task was simple: avoid defeat and become 'The Invincibles'.

In English football, the moniker 'The Invincibles' had been used to refer to the Preston North End team of 1889, managed by Major William Sudell, who were the only team to have completed an English league campaign unbeaten (they did not lose a cup game either). It was a record that had stood for 125 years and Arsenal were now just 90 minutes away from matching it.

Henry's twenty-nine league goals (plus nine in the cups) had gone some way to preserving Arsenal's run, and having surged ahead in the race for the Premiership Golden Boot award, he also had his eye on the equivalent European prize. On the same day that Arsenal met already-relegated Leicester City, his closest challengers, Ailton of Werder Bremen (twenty-seven goals) and Djibril Cissé of Auxerre (twenty-four goals), were both in action across the channel in their respective side's penultimate league games. But first and foremost, all eyes were on Highbury to see if Arsenal could make history.

Team: Lehmann, Lauren, Campbell, Toure, Cole, Ljungberg (87), Vieira, Gilberto, Pires (70), Henry, Bergkamp (82)
Subs: Edu (70), Reyes (82), Keown (87)

With Leicester City already having lost their fight for Premiership survival, any risk that Arsenal would relinquish their unbeaten record against them seemed minimal, and the resultant lack of tension created a party atmosphere at Highbury ahead of the game.

But despite their doomed fate, Leicester were not lacking in effort, and as their confidence grew they stunned Arsenal by taking the lead with 25 minutes gone, when Sinclair's cross found Dickov unmarked at the far post and he headed home.

With their record under threat, Arsenal pressed forward, but Arsenal went into the dressing room 1-0 down. Years later, Henry recalled the atmosphere during that half-time break and the difficulty the team had in staying motivated after securing the League title:

> You still have six or five games to go and I remember the boss coming in every morning saying 'guys you are maybe going to be able to something amazing. Are you realising?' We were like 'we're champions man, come on!' It's like a boxer, a boxer doesn't go in the ring just to have fun. You go out there to kill and that was our mentality [...] Suddenly I remember Patrick [Vieira] looking at me and he was like 'There is no fight, I need to have the fight, I need to know that we need to get some points.' We were not realising what was happening. They [Leicester] go 1-0 up and suddenly you wake up and hope it won't be too late, because you know in this type of game you can hit the crossbar or the post and you can never come back.

Thankfully, the players reacted like a team that knew they couldn't let slip such a unique opportunity, and within a minute of the restart they were level. Sinclair clumsily hauled down Cole in the box and after the referee pointed to the spot Henry stepped up and sent Walker the wrong way for his 30th goal of the season and 39th in total, nudging himself further ahead of the chasing pack for the European Golden Boot.

After 66 minutes, with the unbeaten record within touching distance, Bergkamp unlocked Leicester's defence with a stunning piece of vision, providing a slide-rule pass for Vieira who dribbled around Walker and slid the ball into an empty net.

As Arsenal closed the game out, Keown was brought on as a substitute to ensure he had played enough games to earn a League title winner's medal and his appearance was greeted by huge cheers. Back in September, when Arsenal met Manchester United at Old Trafford, the defender had been involved in an incident with Dutch striker Van Nilstelrooy that had immediately proffered him hero status among Arsenal fans.

Deep into injury time and with the score at 0-0, the striker, already a deeply unpopular player among the Arsenal ranks, missed a penalty that would have given Man United victory. At the final whistle, Van Nistelrooy was confronted by several Arsenal players, including Keown, who jumped in the air and landed with a thump on the Dutchman's back, screaming in his face in a moment of unrestrained *schadenfreude*. The result would be as close as Arsenal came to losing during the entire season and the image of Keown's triumphant gloating – thought it would cost him a £20,000 fine and three-match ban – became a symbol of the squad's mental strength.

So here we were, eight months later, with the club on the brink of taking their place in history. When the final whistle came it was almost anti-climactic, with the players seemingly unsure of how to react – typical, we are told by sports psychologists, of moments of great achievement being followed by a melancholic 'come-down'. But they would have the rest of their lives to reflect on the enormity of what they had achieved in the season that they became The Invincibles.

After the game, Wenger was asked whether this was as good as it gets.

Well, to improve on this in the championship is nearly impossible, but we can win new trophies. I still have problems to realise what we have achieved. I can only say how proud I am of my players.

Arsenal 4 Charlton 0
Premier League
2 October 2004

The Invincibles of 2003/04 were always going to be a hard act to follow, but as the following season progressed Arsenal were doing their utmost to maintain the extraordinary standards they had set. Entering October, they had gone forty-seven consecutive league games unbeaten, stretching all the way back to May 2003, and were playing with a panache that had characterised the entire remarkable run.

For Henry, the disappointment of France's early elimination from the 2004 European Championships was lessened by his consistently excellent club form and he had been an ever-present since the start of the season, scoring four goals in August alone.

It was not just Henry who had carried over the previous season's form but the entire team. Writing in *The Guardian*, David Lacey compared them to a legendary figure from another sport:

> For most of the Premiership taking on Arsenal at present must be rather like facing Muhammad Ali in his prime. No amount of pre-planning or studious ringcraft can prepare opponents for the bewildering combinations of jabs, left hooks and right crosses, the speed of their counterpunching or the balletic grace of their footwork.

Such lyrical waxing was now the norm, and Arsenal's home game with Charlton, which preceded a two-week break for a double header of World Cup qualifiers, was another opportunity to add to their illustrious body of work.

Team: Lehmann, Lauren, Toure, Campbell, Clichy, Ljungberg (49), Vieira, Fabregas (82), Reyes, Bergkamp, Henry (82)
Subs: Pennant (49), Flamini (82), Van Persie (82)

Arsenal had the best of the first half an hour and moved ahead on 33 minutes. Bergkamp drew Kiely out to meet the Dutchman on the edge of the box and, with the keeper stranded, he delivered an inch-perfect cross for Ljungberg, who turned the ball into an unguarded net.

The remainder of the half was relatively uneventful, but within 4 minutes of the restart Henry had added to his bulging portfolio of memorable goals. Reyes played a pass into his feet on the edge of the 6 yard box and, with his back to goal and a Charlton defender up close and personal, Henry produced an improbable back-heel that flew across Kiely and into the bottom corner.

On 69 minutes, two became three with another superlative strike from Henry. Reyes rolled the ball into his partner's path and Henry crashed home an emphatic shot off the underside of the bar from 15 yards. In any other game, it would have been the main talking point, but such was the impudence of his first goal that his second is barely remembered.

Reyes added his name to the scoresheet 2 minutes later, drilling a low first-time effort across Kiely, and Arsenal had stretched their unbeaten run to forty-eight games with a comprehensive victory.

Inevitably, all of the post-match talk centred around that Henry goal. 'I don't think it was the back-heel that was difficult,' said Arsène Wenger, 'but it was difficult to analyse the thing to do. Thierry is so quick to understand what's happening around him and provide the right technical response.'

Charlton manager Alan Curbishley went even further and proclaimed Henry as the world's foremost striker. 'When he scores goals like that people have to sit back and admire him,' he said. 'Without doubt in the last two years he's the best forward there is.'

It was Henry's capacity for invention that perhaps best illustrated his genius. Just when you thought you'd see it all, he would add something new to the footballing vocabulary, with few better examples than his moment of audacity against Charlton.

32

Republic of Ireland 0 France 1
World Cup Qualifier
7 September 2005

When the draw was made for the 2006 World Cup qualifiers it looked as if France had been dealt a relatively kind hand. Placed in a group with Switzerland, Israel, the Republic of Ireland, Cyprus and the Faroe Islands, they went into the campaign as firm favourites under the helm of Raymond Domenech, who had been appointed coach following their disappointing quarter-final exit from the 2004 European Championships.

But three goalless draws, all at home, in their opening five matches erased any expectations of an easy ride through to the finals in Germany the following summer and they went into their away fixture with Ireland with their hopes of qualification precariously balanced.

Domenech was sufficiently concerned that he attempted to persuade several players to come out of international retirement , the most high profile of whom was Zidane. The thirty-three-year-old had hung up his French boots after the 2004 Euros, but to great excitement agreed to return to help his country out of their rut, making his competitive comeback in a 3-0 home win against the Faroe Islands, just six days before their crunch match in Ireland.

Henry's only goal in the qualifiers so far had been the second in a 2-0 away victory in Cyprus almost a year earlier. But he had started the season for Arsenal in good form, scoring three goals in August alone, and was now within touching distance of the club's goal-scoring record, with just two goals needed to overtake Ian Wright's total of 185. However, ahead of the Ireland game he was carrying a groin injury and even if he started was not expected to last the full 90 minutes.

There was another Arsenal connection that promised to add spice to the match and that was the rekindling of one of English football's greatest rivalries. Going head-to-head in midfield would be Henry's Arsenal

1. Arsenal's Thierry Henry reacts during their Champions League second leg semi-final match against Villarreal, 25 April 2006, at El Madrigal stadium in Villarreal, Spain. The game ended in a 0-0 draw with Arsenal advancing to the final after a first leg 1-0 win. (*AP Photo/Tomohiko Suzui*)

2. Arsenal midfielder Jack Wilshere, centre, is tackled by New York Red Bulls forward Thierry Henry, right, in front of Red Bulls defender Roy Miller during the first half of an international friendly soccer game on 26 June 2014. (AP Photo/Adam Hunger)

Above: 3. Arsenal's Thierry Henry fights for the ball with CSKA Moscow Aleksei Berezutsky (*right*) and Yuri Zhirkov (*centre*) during their Group G Champions League soccer match in Moscow, 17 October 2006. (*AP Photo/Sergey Ponomarev*)

Left: 4. The statue of Henry outside Emirates Stadium. (*Courtesy of GrahamC99, Flickr*)

Opposite: 5. Thierry Henry, making a play on the ball midfield versus Real Salt Lake. (*Courtesy of Drew Dies, Flickr*)

6. Emirates Stadium. *(Courtesy of Ronnie MacDonald, Flickr)*

7. The statue of Henry outside Emirates Stadium. (*Courtesy of Ronnie MacDonald, Flickr*)

teammate Vieira and Manchester United's fearsome competitor Keane. Vieira had by now departed England to play for Juventus in Italy, but images of the pair at each other's throats were still fresh in the memory.

Team: Coupet, Sagnol (89), Thuram, Boumsong, Gallas, Makelele, Wiltord, Vieira, Dhorasoo, Zidane (69), Henry (75)
Subs: Malouda (69), Cisse (75), Givet (89)

With both teams knowing they could ill afford to lose, the early moments of the match were predictably cagey, but in the 8th minute Zidane nearly marked his comeback with a free kick that was brilliantly saved by Ireland goalkeeper Given.

Not to be outdone, within 5 minutes, Ireland midfielder Reid saw his free kick curl around the wall and clip the upright. Keane was then unlucky after being brought down in the box when Thuram appeared to clip his heals, but his penalty appeals were waved away. The Irish pressure continued and Morrison's effort went close before Keane's goal bound shot was deflected away for a corner.

France then created their own chance through Makelele, also lured out of international retirement, who saw his shot fly wide following some trickery on the edge of the box, but Ireland were standing firm. France's frustration was evidenced when Zidane was booked for kicking Dunne, who had just dispossessed him.

Vieira's nemesis Keane created a good chance for Ireland after 35 minutes, when he rolled a free kick to Carr, whose shot was blocked by Sagnol and deflected for a corner. Just before half-time, Vieira volleyed a headed Irish clearance from 20 yards but was just off target.

France began to get on top after the break and their pressure told after 67 minutes thanks to a superb goal by Henry. Wiltord controlled the ball on the edge of the Irish box but lost possession, only for Henry to nip in and deftly curl the ball into the far corner of Given's net.

Ireland went in search of an equaliser and won a couple of free-kicks in quick succession that came to nothing. Zidane was then forced off with an injury and was followed by Henry, whose groin problem had begun to take its toll.

But in spite of a late aerial bombardment from Ireland, France held on for a crucial victory that allowed them a fraction of breathing space in their quest for World Cup qualification. And the man they had to thank was Henry, who, in spite of a debilitating injury, found the resources to produce a goal of such importance that it made a mockery of claims that he was not the man for the big occasion. Henry and France were on their way to Germany.

33

Sparta Prague 0 Arsenal 2
Champions League Group Match
18 October 2005

Arsenal travelled to Czech club Sparta Prague knowing that a win would virtually assure them of a place in the last sixteen of the Champions League. With two victories from their opening two games in the competition, the club's European fortunes had been in stark contrast with their Premiership exertions, which had seen them lose three games in their first eight fixtures.

Already, their ability to win back the title they last won two years earlier was being sternly questioned, and to make matters worse, their star man (and now club captain after Vieira's summer departure to Juventus) Henry had missed the last seven games with a groin injury and remained a doubt for the trip to Prague.

Henry's absence had not only hindered Arsenal's early title challenge, but also curtailed his efforts to become Arsenal's record goalscorer. His three strikes for the season so far had nudged him tantalisingly close to Ian Wright's record of 185 goals for the club, which had stood since September 1997, and he was now only a single goal away from matching Wright's total.

According to his biographer, Philippe Auclair, Henry had been a fan of Wright since he scored against his childhood team Paris St Germain during Arsenal's 1993/94 European Cup Winners' Cup campaign. Henry would later describe watching Wright on television back in France when he was a budding young Monaco apprentice.

> I said to myself, 'he's no bigger than me, no faster, no more muscular, but he scores more goals'. I watched him closely. He put 100 per cent into everything. When he called for a pass, he shouted at the top of his voice, and when he got it, he'd smack it into the back of the net.

As legend has it, on the day Henry signed for Arsenal, the club's vice-chairman, David Dein, handed him a video of Wright's goals with the message 'This is what you've got to do'. Now, 303 matches and just over six seasons later, he was on the brink of accomplishing Dein's fanciful challenge.

But even if his injury meant Henry would have to wait a little longer, he could at least take comfort in the fact that nothing barring a disaster could now prevent him becoming Arsenal's greatest ever goalscorer. Furthermore, it was not only a matter of 'when' not 'if', but also of 'how many'. Aged twenty-eight, he had at least another five years at the highest level and could conceivably smash the record beyond reach of anyone for decades or even centuries to come. Whether, of course, those years would be played in the red and white of Arsenal remained to be seen.

Team: Lehmann, Lauren, Toure, Cygan, Clichy, Fabregas (89), Flamini, Gilberto, Reyes (15), Pires, Van Persie (73)
Subs: Henry (15), Eboue (73), Owusu-Abeyie (89)

The game was lent an unusual feel by the absence of half of Sparta Prague's usually vociferous support, the result of punishment for racial abuse being heard in the crowd during their previous European home match against Ajax. It would of course be deeply fitting if a black player could deliver further penance, and the possibility of that happening increased when Henry was surprisingly named on Arsenal's substitutes bench.

Prior to the game, Arsenal boss Arsène Wenger had hinted that he may give Henry 30 minutes action, but his hand was forced when Reyes sustained bruised ribs in a clattering challenge and he was instead compelled to introduce Henry with just 15 minutes played.

If he was still feeling his injury, he was doing a good job of concealing it and just 3 minutes after coming on, he almost scored a sensational goal, chesting a long ball down before swivelling and firing a volley that was deflected just over the bar. It was some introduction, and made even more remarkable by the fact that he hadn't even warmed up before coming on, instead doing his stretching exercises on the pitch during quiet passages of play. But there was even better to come.

On 21 minutes, Henry ran on to a long ball from Toure and trapped it with the outside of his right boot on the edge of the penalty area. With four Sparta defenders in close attention, he checked, weighed up his options and curled a delicious shot with the outside of his right food into the far corner. Despite the significance of the goal, Henry marked the moment in typical fashion, with a furrowed brow, slapping the Arsenal crest on his shirt as his teammates came to congratulate him. Having not expected to even be on the pitch, the lack of a choreographed celebration was perhaps no surprise. But the record had been cast: Henry was now Arsenal's joint top goalscorer of all time.

The remainder of the half was played out with little to speak of by way of chances and the second period began in a similar vein. With Arsenal dropping deep and inviting pressure, Sparta were enjoying the bulk of the possession but Lehmann had to make just one telling save, pushing over a long-range effort from Kisel.

At the other end, Blazek was equally underemployed, a shot from Fabregas the only time he was called into action until he picked the ball out of the net on 74 minutes. The goal wrapped up Arsenal's crucial victory and propelled Henry into the history books.

It came when Arsenal won a loose ball in midfield, which was collected by Pires on the right flank. Just inside Sparta's half, he looked up and saw Henry between the two centre backs with his arm aloft and curled a 30-yard ball that arced behind the defenders and into space for the striker to run into. It was an incredible pass and Henry treated it with the respect it deserved, controlling it, steadying himself and slotting the ball home for his 186th Arsenal goal.

Henry turned and trotted with his back to goal towards the corner of the pitch, cajoling his teammates to come and join him. If ever there was a time to drop the angry veneer, then surely this was it, and Henry obliged by breaking into a beaming smile.

'It was a strange situation for me because I wasn't even going to travel,' Henry said after the game, 'I was a bit sad because I wanted to do it at Highbury, but there we go. I called my teammates and I just wanted to celebrate with them because without them I wouldn't have been able to do it.'

'When you play as a striker you need to be instinctive,' he continued,

I tried one just before after I came on and the defender just flicked it with his head and I said to myself 'If I have another one I will try to smash it in.' And I guess it was a sign because Wrighty used to score some smashing goals [...] I said to some of the guys afterwards, it's important also that the goals were important in the game. Sometimes if you do it [break a record] and your team doesn't win it can be a bit flat. Everything happened so quick, I wasn't meant to travel, I wasn't meant to play. I guess it's fate. I can't find my words.

It was left to Arsène Wenger to sum up Henry's achievement:

First you have to say he beat the record in a relatively short time and also he's not a typical goalscorer. He's an all-round player, not the guy who's hunting in the box to score goals. So it's unexplainable how the guy who is not really interested in scoring only goals can score so many [...] I think he's not only gone into the history of the club, he's gone into the history of football. Don't forget that he is twenty-eight only. When Ian Wright beat the record he was thirty-three or thirty-four, so he has a long time in front of him. There is a lot more to come from him.

34

Real Madrid 0 Arsenal 1
Champions League Knockout Stage
21 February 2006

More than two months had passed since the end of the Champions League group stages and Arsenal's league form had been patchy to say the least. Five defeats in twelve games had struck them firmly out of the running for the Premiership title and to compound things they had also exited both domestic cups.

With the Champions League now their only hope of salvation, their prospects of winning the trophy (something no London club had ever done) seemed to diminish when they were drawn against Spanish giants Real Madrid in the two-legged knockout stages. Boasting among their ranks Zidane, Beckham, Ronaldo, Roberto Carlos and Robinho, it was for good reason that they were known by the nickname 'The Galacticos'.

Ahead of the first leg in Madrid, coach Arsène Wenger spoke of his belief that the match could provide a springboard to lift them out of the doldrums. But with a total of eight players on the treatment table, mostly defenders, it was tempting to think that even Wenger did not truly believe his team could overcome this sizeable hurdle.

One factor in their favour amid their domestic struggles was the continued good form of their greatest ever goalscorer, who had notched eight goals in his past ten games. Henry had been strongly linked with Real Madrid's arch rivals Barcelona the previous summer and there had been suggestions that they would return the following close season with a more concrete effort to lure him away from Highbury. Whether true or not, this represented another opportunity for Henry to show his worth on one of football's most prestigious stages: the hallowed turf of Estadio Santiago Bernabéu.

Team: Lehmann, Eboue, Senderos, Toure, Flamini, Ljungberg, Gilberto, Fabregas (89), Hleb (76), Reyes (80), Henry
Subs: Reyes (76), Diaby (80), Song (89)

As if Arsenal's task wasn't hard enough, they lined up with three of their four first-choice defenders missing and without a recognised left-back, forcing midfielder Flamini to cover. Wenger also caused a surprise by starting Reyes on the left of a five man midfield, with Pires dropping to the bench. Midfield prodigy Fabregas, a graduate of the Barcelona youth team, also made the starting eleven.

Nevertheless, Wenger's under-strength side performed with great maturity in the first 45 minutes, and as early as the second minute they could have gone ahead when Henry set up Reyes, whose shot was saved.

The early chances kept on coming for Arsenal and after 9 minutes Henry should have scored when he rose unmarked to meet Reyes' cross, but headed off target. Half-time arrived and there was little doubt which was the happier team. Far from being over-awed by their illustrious opponents, Arsenal had taken the game to Real Madrid and on the infrequent occasions the Spanish side attacked, the Gunners' makeshift defence had stood firm.

If anyone expected the Real onslaught to arrive in earnest in the second half, they could not have been more wrong. Just 2 minutes after the restart, Fabregas played a short pass to Henry who had dropped back into the centre circle. As Ronaldo chased back, Henry turned on his heels and when the duo came into contact the Brazilian striker simply bounced off him. Real defender Mejia then lunged in but Henry powered past him with ease. Next it was Guti's turn and Henry skipped that challenge too. Suddenly he was powering into the penalty box and as Ramos came across to launch a last ditch tackle, Henry slid a left-footed shot beyond Casillas and into the far corner.

Henry celebrated by running towards the 3,500-strong visiting support with his arms out wide. Aesthetically, it brought to mind his effort against Spurs at Highbury in 2002 when he ran from within his own half, but on this occasion the opponents were far from north London lightweights. This was a world-class goal against world-class opposition on a world-class stage.

For the rest of the half, Arsenal remained a danger and substitute Diaby almost marked his entry with a goal after 89 minutes, only for Casillas to save at his feet. Then deep into injury time, Beckham nearly created a last-gasp equaliser for Ronaldo but he failed to connect with an inviting cross.

The final whistle went and Arsenal became the first English side to beat Real Madrid in the Spanish capital. They had also secured an improbable first leg lead, scoring a crucial 'away' goal that now gave them an eminently realistic chance of progressing to the quarter-finals. Never mind their Premier League worries – if they could beat Real Madrid they could achieve anything. And no player better symbolised this dream than the chief architect of their victory: Henry.

35

Arsenal 2 Juventus 0
Champions League Quarter-Final
1st Leg, 28 March 2006

To Arsenal fans today, the names of Eboue, Senderos and Toure do not necessarily conjure up memories of accomplished defending, but as unlikely as it now seems, back in March 2006 they were part of a back four that had not conceded a goal for 559 minutes of Europe football. As they prepared to face Italian giants Juventus in the Champions League quarter-finals, they were just 100 minutes from beating Ajax's European shut-out record.

Arsenal had already caused ripples across Europe's premier competition after knocking out Real Madrid in the previous round, a Henry-inspired victory in Madrid followed by a 0-0 draw at Highbury. But their next opponents appeared almost as tough, with Juventus sitting eight points clear at the top of Serie A.

Nevertheless, Arsenal's vanquishing of Real Madrid had gained them newfound respect and, as England's last representatives in the competition, they were only marginal underdogs ahead of the first leg. Their Premiership form had also picked up, having won their last three league games, giving them hope of a top-four finish. It still seemed a long way to the Champions League final, but they had momentum on their side and in Henry a striker widely considered the world's best.

Henry also provided the tie with a noteworthy subplot. His poor spell at Juventus had led to him seeking sanctuary at Arsenal and although he had already faced his old team back in 2001 for Arsenal, scoring an eye-catching free kick in a 3-1 victory, this was another chance to bury his Turin demons even deeper.

There was also the small matter of the return of Vieira, Henry's predecessor as club captain and an Arsenal legend after nine hugely successful years at the club. Having been linked with moves away from the club seemingly every summer, he eventually joining Juventus in 2006. His first game back would see him go head to head with one of his Highbury protégés, the Spanish midfielder Fabregas.

Ahead of the game, Arsène Wenger was keen to stress the importance of the first leg: 'The first game of the two ties determines qualification. That psychological print in the heads of the two teams is always decisive.'

Team: Lehmann, Eboue, Senderos, Toure, Flamini, Pires, Fabregas, Hleb, Gilberto, Reyes (82), Henry
Subs: Van Persie (82)

Juventus looked to stamp their physicality on the midfield early in proceedings, with Vieira giving away a free-kick for a foul on Fabregas inside 2 minutes. The same duo were involved in the first chance of the game on 16 minutes when Febregas scuttled away from his former teammate, latching onto Pires' backheel only to drag his shot wide.

On 38 minutes, Vieira took on the mantle of pantomime villain when Fabregas (who else?) scythed him down. As Vieira stayed grounded, the Arsenal fans responded with boos, but you could tell their hearts were not in it. Their affection for the big Frenchman still burned strongly.

But Vieira's night was about to get worse. Five minutes before halftime, he dithered on the halfway line and was dispossessed with a slide tackle by the unlikely figure of Pires. He passed to Henry who in turn found Fabregas and the Spaniard took a couple of touches before wrong-footing Juventus goalkeeper Buffon with a low shot that trickled into the net.

A minute after Fabregas' goal, Henry went close with a shot from a tight angle, and as the half-time whistle arrived the home team were firmly in the ascendancy.

Early in the second half, Arsenal began piling on the pressure, but had to wait until the 69th minute for the crucial second goal to arrive. Fabregas collected a neat pass deep into the penalty box and as Buffon came out of goal he cut the ball back to Henry, who controlled and fired into an empty net for his 27th goal of the season.

Vieira was then booked for a tackle on Reyes (meaning he would be suspended for the second leg) as Arsenal stroked the ball about with ease. In the final minutes Camoranesi and Zebina both received their second yellow cards and Juventus ended the match in shambolic fashion with just nine men on the pitch.

Arsenal's clean sheet meant they had now gone seven matches without conceding in the Champions League, equalling the record set by AC Milan the previous season. It was a remarkable achievement given their injury problems, and they were now tantalisingly close to their first ever Champions League semi-final appearance.

Nevertheless, after the game Henry was keen to nip any risk of complacency in the bud:

> I will tell you how important this result is when we have gone over there. Even after the second goal I was shouting at people to do their jobs and not to get carried away. A team like Juve can kill you in two minutes. That is why I was a bit vocal. We had a good night and you could say they had a bad night. But they could have a good one over there. I know some of the players there and they are capable of doing it.

Arsenal followed up their comprehensive first leg victory with a 0-0 draw in Turin, in which Henry gave Juventus a torrid time for almost the whole match. As sensible as Henry's call for caution may have been, there was now little doubt that Arsenal were genuine contenders to win the trophy. If there was a suspicion that the Real Madrid victory had been a fluke, all observers could now agree that Arsenal were the real deal.

36

Arsenal 1 Tottenham Hotspur 1
Premier League
22 April 2006

So consumed had Arsenal been by their unlikely Champions League progress that the fact they were playing out their final season at Highbury (their home for ninety-three years) had almost become a side-story. That summer they would move into Emirates Stadium, a brand-spanking new 60,000 capacity stadium that the club hoped would allow them to compete financially with the cream of world football.

The season had been sprinkled with significant landmarks, all building up to that final game at the famous old stadium against Wigan Athletic to be played on Sunday 7 May. One such milestone was Highbury's final ever north London derby, but ahead of the match with Tottenham, a brief glance at the league table would reveal far more at stake than sentiment.

The two clubs were in the grips of a furious battle to finish in fourth place – the final league position that would ensure them Champion League qualification. Tottenham were in pole position and victory at Highbury would be enough to see them over the line. While Arsenal could certainly not afford to lose, even a draw would mean their fate remained in Tottenham's hands.

But as well as being vulnerable from a points perspective, Arsenal were also caught in a psychological dilemma. Three days prior to the Tottenham game, they had beaten Spanish side Villarreal 1-0 in the first leg of the Champions League semi-finals. They were now just 90 minutes from reaching the final for the first time in the club's history.

The problem was that the intensity of their mid-week game had taken its toll to such an extent that Arsène Wenger decided to start against Spurs with both Fabregas and Henry on the bench. Wenger had been criticised earlier in the month for resting Henry for Arsenal's visit to Manchester United, which they lost 2-0, but Arsenal fans would once again be asked to trust his judgement. The truth was that it was not so much that he was prioritising Europe over the league, but mitigating the risk of Arsenal imploding in both. Just three days after the Spurs game they would travel to Spain for the second leg and, quite simply, something had to give.

Team: Lehmann, Djourou, Toure, Senderos (54), Flamini, Pires, Gilberto, Diaby (62), Reyes, Adebayor, Van Persie (62)
Subs: Eboue (54), Fabregas (62), Henry (62)

With Henry on the bench, Arsenal started with Adebayor, who had signed from French club Monaco in the January transfer window. Despite four goals in twelve appearances, he had not yet convinced fans that he was the striker to replace Henry should he depart in the summer, as many were now predicting.

After weathering some early pressure, Tottenham began to trouble Arsenal, largely through the right-wing threat of Aaron Lennon, but they saved the best of an impressive first-half for the last minute, when Carrick beat three Arsenal challenges and Lehmann before shooting into the side netting from a tight angle.

In the second half, Arsenal gradually began to work their way into the game and with about half an hour to go Van Persie was presented with a great chance when he beat the offside trap but lifted his shot over Robinson and wide.

With the game in the balance, Wenger introduced his two key men from the bench. But far from providing Arsenal with added impetus, just 4 minutes after their introduction Tottenham took the lead in controversial fashion.

Arsenal's Gilberto and Eboue both challenged for a ball in midfield, injuring themselves in the process. With both prostrate on the ground, the Arsenal players paused, expecting Tottenham to put the ball out of play so their teammates could receive treatment. But instead they continued moving the ball forward until Davids was released on the left. He slid a perfect ball across for Keane to tap in at the far post.

As Keane celebrated, Arsenal's players, including goalkeeper Lehmann, unleashed their anger on Davids, who they felt should have done the sporting thing, while on the touchline Wenger and Spurs counterpart Martin Jol squared up against each other and had to be restrained by the fourth official.

Once the dust settled and play resumed, Arsenal nearly equalised soon after when Henry crossed for Reyes, whose volley was pushed wide by Robinson, but as the minutes ticked on the unthinkable was becoming ever more real. Arsenal were on the verge of losing the last ever game against their bitter rivals at Highbury and vanquishing their top four status in the process.

With 6 minutes left, Arsenal looked to be running out of ideas and needed something special to avoid this hellish scenario from coming true. Step forward the one man on the pitch who, more than any other, had a sense for the occasion.

A long ball was punted forward and controlled neatly by Adebayor, who turned and powered down the left wing. After evading Lennon, he cut inside and slipped a pass into the penalty box for a marauding Henry to run on to. Henry took one touch and almost in the same movement flicked an audacious shot with the outside of his right foot, which took Robinson by surprise and nestled in the corner.

Henry celebrated by running the length of the pitch towards the away fans, just as he did after his mesmerising goal from his own half against the same opponents in 2002. On this occasion he resisted taunting them quite so enthusiastically, perhaps because a draw was not of huge use to Arsenal. The only way they could now finish fourth was to win their last three games and hope Tottenham dropped points in at least one of their two remaining fixtures.

But there was no escaping that, on this day of all days, for Arsenal to avoid defeat also had symbolic value. Henry's brilliance had saved Arsenal from a black mark against the memory of their final ever season at Highbury and in doing so added further gloss to his legend.

A couple of days later, *The Guardian* newspaper neatly summarised the impact of Henry's substitution, writing that he 'psychologically boosts his team while deflating opponents'. But Wenger knew that his decision to start him on the bench would still be used as a stick to beat him and, after the game, jumped to his own defence:

I don't believe that it was a team selection problem, it was a physical problem. We play every three days and people maybe don't realise that but you know you can sometimes suffer. It's difficult to imagine how much tension is in the Champions League games and you know you could have a flat half, no matter who started the game. It is a real battle at that level, where everybody goes 100 per cent for it. You have to recover as well and of course people will criticise because Thierry Henry didn't play.

Henry himself confessed to being disappointed not to start, but acknowledged that it may have been the sensible decision. 'I don't like it but you have to accept it. If you want to be fresh and sharp then somewhere along the line you have to take a break from games.'

He also elaborated on why he and his teammates had been so angry after Tottenham's contentious goal:

I think you can understand why we were upset. It's an important game, not only for fourth spot but it's the last derby game at Highbury and that's why we felt we were being cheated. There's been times when players have clashed heads and I could have scored. But I've never been like that. If I want to beat someone or win a game, I want to do it because of me and nothing else.

37

Arsenal 4 Wigan Athletic 2
Premier League
7 May 2006

If there had been any hope that Arsenal's Highbury swansong could be played out in an atmosphere of nostalgic reflection, then those prospects were well and truly dashed as they prepared to play Wigan Athletic in their final ever game at the famous stadium.

With Tottenham in fourth place, a point ahead of Arsenal in the table, the Gunners were on the brink of missing out on Champions League qualification for the first time in nine years and were reliant on their local rivals dropping points at West Ham if they were to avoid that fate. If the Hammers granted them that favour, Arsenal would then need to better Tottenham's result to secure fourth place.

The tension of the situation was eased only a fraction by the fact that ten days later Arsenal would be appearing in their first ever Champions League final in Paris, which they had reached after beating Villarreal 1-0 on aggregate in the semi-finals. If they could land the coveted trophy, they would automatically qualify for the next year's competition, rendering their result against Wigan academic. The main obstacle to this scenario was that their opponents, Barcelona, were widely considered one of the greatest club sides in history.

It meant that they simply had to go all out for victory against Wigan and hope that Tottenham would implode in a way that had become something of a forte for them in recent years. As it turned out, it would be explosions of an altogether less savoury variety that would prove their undoing, after a dodgy lasagne served up by their hotel chef before the game laid low half of the Tottenham side. Never shy about contriving imaginative ways to humiliate themselves, this was perhaps a new nadir and, as far as Arsenal fans were concerned, it would have taken a heart of stone not to laugh.

First, though, Arsenal had their own stomach-clenching 90 minutes to negotiate, and it would be played with the weight of ninety-three years of history on their shoulders. To add to the emotion of the day, four of the club's most distinguished players were likely to be playing their last games for the club, with Bergkamp and Pires both expected to leave after Arsenal refused to give them more than a one-year contract extension. A more acrimonious departure was expected to be left-back Cole, who had also rejected Arsenal's contract offer and had upset fans after been caught meeting with Chelsea bosses about a possible transfer to west London.

Also on the prospective exit list was newly-crowned PFA Player of the Year Henry, who continued to be strongly linked with a big money summer move, with Champions League final opponents Barcelona mooted as his likely destination.

Team: Lehmann, Eboue, Campbell, Toure, Cole, Hleb (79), Fabregas, Gilberto, Reyes (79), Pires (74), Henry
Subs: Ljungberg (74), Bergkamp (79), Van Persie (79)

Decked out in the commemorative redcurrant shirts they had worn all season in honour of their first season at Highbury in 1913, Arsenal started the game brightly and nearly scored when Reyes dragged a pass back for Henry, whose shot was blocked by Scharner.

After 10 minutes, they took the lead. A cross from Fabregas was met by Gilberto, whose header was saved, only to rebound to Pires, who forced the ball home at the second attempt. Moments later, the excitement levels rose when news filtered through that West Ham had taken the lead against Tottenham. So far, the footballing gods were sticking to the script, but Wigan were about to rip it to shreds.

Two minutes after Arsenal's opener, Thompson swung in a Wigan free-kick that Gilberto left at the near post and with no one there to clear, Scharner slipped in and tucked the ball into the net for the equaliser. As half-time approached, Wigan threw another sizeable spanner in the works by taking the lead. Thomson lined up a free-kick from 40 yards out – far enough for Lehmann to decide a wall was not required – and the Wigan player angled a fierce curled drive that took the goalkeeper by a surprise.

Arsenal responded in the only acceptable fashion for such a high-stakes situation, fighting terrier-like for every ball, and it was such determination that brought them a quick equaliser. Hleb won possession deep inside Wigan's half and passed to Pires who played a first time ball through to Henry which he controlled before slotting home.

Almost at the same moment, Tottenham equalised against West Ham, leaving matters finely balanced at the half-time break. As it stood, Tottenham would finish fourth, but with 45 minutes still to play there was ample time for more twists and turns.

Eleven minutes into the second half, Thompson woefully under-hit a back-pass and the worst man possible (from Wigan's perspective) was onto it like a flash. Henry calmly walked the ball around Wigan goalkeeper Pollitt and passed it into the empty net.

Arsenal now had a fragile grip on fourth place, but with Tottenham needing just one goal to swing the pendulum back in their favour, they could not yet relax. They reacted accordingly and very nearly added to their lead through a header from Fabregas. Then, with fourteen minutes left, Arsenal virtually assured themselves victory with the goal that has gone down in the history books as the last ever scored at Highbury.

It came from the penalty spot and it wrapped up a hat-trick for Henry, who slotted home before falling to his knees and kissing the turf in front of the North Bank. The stand had been redeveloped from terraces in the 1990s as part of the drive to modernise football stadia in the UK, but it still represented the collective heartbeat of the club's support. For the final goal the stadium would ever see to be scored at that end, by perhaps their greatest ever player, was deeply fitting.

As the celebrations died down, news arrived that West Ham had regained the lead against Tottenham with just 10 minutes remaining at Upton Park. Spurs now needed two goals to reclaim fourth place and with their side already depleted by illness it was too much to ask.

The final whistle went at both grounds and Arsenal had secured their place among Europe's elite for the ninth year running, ensuring they would leave Highbury in fine spirits and with a Champions League final to look forward to as well.

Amid the choreographed party that followed, including live music by Roger Daltry of The Who and a parade of former players, Henry, Cole and Pires all sat together in the centre circle contemplating the enormity of the occasion. With all three possibly leaving the club that summer, it was a scene of mixed emotions for Arsenal fans and probably the protagonists too.

During the celebrations, as Henry was presented with the Premiership Golden Boot for his twenty-seven goals, the fans started chanting for the club to 'sign him up'. With his name ringing around the ground, the love for him never more apparent, he surveyed the scene and one wondered about the effect these moments were having on his thoughts about the future. Long after most of his team mates had gone home, he reluctantly walked off the pitch.

'I think it was a bit strange everyone left like that,' he said after the match, referring to the fact that most of his teammates had disappeared down the tunnel as soon as the pre-match party came to an end. He added,

But at the end of the day I think some of the players in the team are really young and haven't won a lot here, so maybe it was less special for them. But Dennis [Bergkamp] is still here, I'm still here, Ashley [Cole] was there. People who played a long time here were sitting there enjoying it. Me and Ashley were saying to ourselves 'we don't want to leave'. Highbury is just a special place.

Was this the end of the road for Henry at Arsenal, or had he merely reached a new junction from which he would guide them on a new journey of just a few 100 yards towards their new 60,000 capacity super-stadium?

38

Barcelona 2 Arsenal 1
Champions League Final
17 May 2006

Given the undeniable flaws in their squad, it was hard to rationalise Arsenal's progress to the Champions League final, and there were few who truly believed it would herald an era of European domination. With Bergkamp, Campbell, Pires, Cole and Reyes all expected to leave and Henry's future shrouded in doubt, in a way this felt more like the end of an era than the beginning of one.

Granted, a glitzy new stadium was waiting to be occupied, but what purpose moving into an opulent mansion if only to fill it with Ikea furniture? To further complicate matters, Arsenal had taken on major debt to finance the stadium move and there was uncertainty about how competitive they would now be in the transfer market – at least in the medium term.

Throughout the season fans had been discussing the major concerns they feared were just over the horizon. When would they finally buy a worthy replacement for Vieira? Could Hleb do the job of the departing Pires? If Henry was sold, would the money be reinvested or diverted to service the stadium debt?

But for one night only, these questions could wait. Arsenal were about to make their first ever appearance in the most prestigious fixture in club football and arguably the biggest match in their history. Not only would winning the trophy correct a notable omission in the club's honours list, but it could also help smooth the period of transition that seemed to be lying ahead.

Having failed to mount a Premiership title challenge, they had at least achieved the next best thing and qualified for the Champions League through their league position (at the expense of Tottenham, much to their delight) ten days earlier. Now only the prospect of silverware hinged on the final against Barcelona, but what glorious silverware it was. Wenger had never won a European trophy, and for some of his players it would be their last chance to do so (in Arsenal colours, at least).

Team: Lehmann, Eboue, Campbell, Toure, Cole, Ljungberg, Fabregas (74), Hleb (85), Gilberto, Pires (20), Henry

Subs: Almunia (20), Flamini (74), Reyes (85)

Arsenal's Champions League run had been built on a remarkably solid defence that had not conceded a goal since their group stage match at Ajax in September, despite often missing three first-choice starters due to injury. But while his patched up back four received most of the plaudits, Arsène Wenger's tactical shift to 4-5-1 was perhaps somewhat overlooked.

With Hleb, Ljungberg and Pires pushing forward to support Henry, the lone striker, and Fabregas and Gilberto offering defensive cover in the middle, it had become his tried and tested formation in Europe and there seemed little reason to fix what wasn't broken in the final. Facing one of the greatest Barcelona sides of all time, complete with Ronaldinho, Eto'o and Deco, this was no time for experimentation.

On no player did Arsenal's European formation put more demands than Henry. 'I had to learn how to play with my back to goal', he would later admit,

> I had to adapt to a way of playing which wasn't naturally me. To play upfront in a 4-5-1 implies a huge amount of mental work: you can tell yourself that you night only get one ball, and that you must make something of it. This was especially difficult for someone like me who needs to touch the ball to feel all right.

But Henry had no one to blame but himself for two early misses that could have given Arsenal a dream start. First he turned in the Barcelona box, only to be denied by the diving Valdes from point-blank range. Then from the resulting short corner, he fired in an angled drive, which was pushed to safety by the Spanish goalkeeper.

Barca responded well and before long Arsenal goalkeeper Lehmann was called into action twice, first saving from Giuly and then Deco. But with 18 minutes gone, the volatile German 'keeper changed the landscape of the game with a reckless misjudgement. As Eto'o bore down on goal, Lehmann came racing out of his area and when the Cameroonian striker tried to go round him, the goalkeeper scythed him down. The loose ball fell to Giuly, who tapped home into an empty net, but the referee had already blown for the free-kick and promptly showed Lehmann the red card for a professional foul.

The sending off not only left Arsenal with the task of facing one of the best passing sides in the world with ten men, but it also had the inadvertent effect of ending the Arsenal career of their fan's favourite Frenchman Pires. With replacement goalkeeper Almunia coming on, an outfield player had to be sacrificed and Wenger chose Pires, based on the fair assumption that Arsenal would need stamina rather than guile over the coming 68-plus minutes. As expected, Pires would leave that summer to join Villareal on a free transfer and it was a sad end to an otherwise highly distinguished seven years at the club.

With their numerical advantage, Barcelona started to take control but were stunned when Arsenal went ahead after 37 minutes. The Gunners were fortunate to be given a free-kick after Eboue tumbled theatrically under a challenge from Puyol, but when Henry floated the free kick in, Campbell headed home emphatically.

Arsenal hung on desperately for the remainder of the first half, with Almunia turning Eto'o's shot onto the post. Their defence had now not conceded a goal for 900 minutes – if they could add a comparatively paltry 45 to that total, they would be Champions of Europe.

Barcelona made a half-time change with Iniesta coming on for the injured Edmilson and the substitute tested Almunia after 51 minutes, with the 'keeper doing well to clutch a shot that skidded off the wet surface.

But Arsenal were still dangerous on the break, with Henry and Fabregas combining to set up Hleb, but he pulled his shot wide.

On 69 minutes, Henry had a glorious chance to double Arsenal's advantage but Valdes saved low down to keep Barcelona's hopes alive. It was to prove the pivotal moment of the game and, in the fullness of time, would perhaps be the single miss of Henry's career that would be remembered beyond his playing days.

Many would use it as evidence that he wasn't a player for the big occasion, but this was always an absurd accusation for a player who consistently scored crucial goals against all kinds of opponents throughout his career. In any case, the miss was eminently forgivable since he must have been physically drained after leading the line with little support for almost an hour.

Henry would later say as much and was in fact far more annoyed with the earlier chance he had failed to convert:

I didn't make the difference. I'll be the first to say that. I've got two big chances. On the second one – not that I'm looking for excuses – we'd been playing with ten men for fifty minutes, and I had nothing left in my socks. But the first one, I have to put it in the net. And I think about it often. It annoys me, because of what the consequences were [...] I always have the feeling I've let me team down if I haven't made a difference. And that's what I felt then.

Whether or not one chooses to criticise Henry for that miss, Arsenal would surely have gone on to win had Henry scored. Instead, with 14 minutes to go, Barcelona broke Arsenal's resistance by forcing an equaliser when former Celtic star Larsson delivered a deft pass into the path of Eto'o (who replays showed to be marginally offside), and he tucked a neat finish past Almunia at the near post.

Six minutes later, substitute Belletti gave Barcelona the lead after being picked out by another neat Larsson pass. Replays once again added salt to Arsenal's wounds, as Belleti's shot looked to be going wide when it hit Almunia on the inside of the foot and ricocheted into the net. It was a killer blow from which Arsenal never recovered.

After full-time, as the Arsenal players lingered on the pitch waiting for the trophy-giving ceremony, Henry stood alongside his coach and could be seen expressing his frustrations. There were so many 'what ifs' to have arisen from the game, it would be pointless even speculating what had irked Henry the most.

But if one was to indulge, one would perhaps consider whether during these moments he realised he couldn't leave the club on such a sour note. Because two days later he announced he would be staying at Arsenal, putting pen to paper on a new four-year deal worth a rumoured £6 million a year (plus a £5 million signing-on fee). It was an mind-boggling figure, but Henry's star was still burning brightly enough to command such remuneration, and so if Arsenal wanted to keep him, they had to pay his market value.

Arsène Wenger clearly thought he was worth every penny, saying he 'had two aims at the start of the week: to win the European Cup and then to make Thierry stay. I only managed one of those but for the future of the club, that's certainly the best one.'

After his re-signing, Arsenal vice-chairman David Dein indirectly confirmed the club had rejected two £50 million offers for Henry from Spanish giants Barcelona and Real Madrid. 'We turned down two world-record deals from Spanish clubs', Dein said. 'You don't have to be a rocket scientist to work out who they were.'

Dein also claimed the chance to influence the next generation of youngsters at Arsenal may have influenced Henry's decision:

He had seen the youngsters emerge after a dark period. We have three teenagers at the World Cup – how many other clubs can say that? The reason they are here is because of Thierry. The first question Theo Walcott asked was 'Will Thierry still be here?' I believe he also knew that if he went to a club like Barcelona or Real Madrid, he would just be a prince. Here he knows he is a king.

With or without King Henry, no one was in any doubt that Arsenal faced a challenging time ahead. History had shown that clubs often struggled after moving stadium, and Arsenal were about to lose some of their most experienced players just at a point when stability was required. Furthermore, while a Russian billionaire was continuing to bankroll London rivals Chelsea, Arsenal were financially straitjacketed by their new stadium. Wenger had prepared for a period of austerity by fast-tracking a number of talented youth players into the first team, but it was a policy that came with significant risk.

After signing his new contract, Henry told *France Football* magazine, 'There's an awful lot of quality in this group, but it is not well exploited yet. I'll take a while – but I've always had this mindset. I hope these youngsters can mature as quickly as possible.'

For now, though, Arsenal would take a backseat. Henry was about to appear in his third World Cup finals.

39

Italy 1 France 1
(Italy Won on Penalties)
World Cup Final, 9 July 2006

The 2005/06 season was a gruelling one for Henry and must have left him with mixed emotions. An impressive thirty-three goals in all competitions, including becoming Arsenal's record goalscorer, continued his upward career trajectory, but there were disappointments too, most notably Arsenal's failure to challenge for the League title followed by their Champions League final defeat to Barcelona.

A keen sentimentalist, Henry was also sad to say goodbye to Highbury ('my garden') as Arsenal prepared to enter the brave new world waiting for them at Emirates Stadium. Nevertheless, he ended the season by signing a new contract at the club, bringing to a close months of speculation about his future laying in Spain.

His immediate prospects, however, would take him to Germany for the 2006 World Cup finals, where France hoped to bounce back from the disappointment of their previous two major tournaments. Their qualifying campaign, which saw them draw their first three home games 0-0 against weaker opposition, did not bode well for their chances but they had been boosted by the return of Zidane, who had come out of international retirement a year earlier and still looked to have plenty to offer.

France coach Raymond Domenech opted for a 4-5-1 formation for the finals, with Henry asked to toil on his own upfront, supported by the young legs of Ribery and Malouda and the experience of Zidane. Having played forty-five matches across the season for Arsenal, it seemed a lot to ask of Henry, not least as many felt he was unsuited to the role of lone frontman.

Repeating the unconvincing form they had shown in qualifying, France stumbled through the group stage, drawing their opening two games against Switzerland and South Korea, teams that on paper they should have beaten.

A goal by Henry, his second of the tournament, in a 2-0 victory over Togo ensured they scraped through to the knockout rounds.

It was at this point that France came alive, dispatching first of Spain, then Brazil and Portugal to reach the final, with Zidane rolling back the years with a series of sublime performances. In the quarter-final against Brazil, it was his free kick to the far post that was met by Henry's right boot to put France through, establishing a curious statistical quirk; it was the only time Zidane directly assisted Henry for a goal in their long international career together. Those of a more cynical disposition suspected that the anomaly hinted at underlying acrimony between the duo.

In a 2013 interview with *France Football* weekly magazine, Henry's biographer Philippe Auclair said he believed that Henry 'suffered from the fact that there was this idea, this theory, that he and Zidane were adversaries, were rivals, with Zizou very much reluctant to pass on the keys of the team to his natural successor, who was of course Thierry'.

Whatever the root cause, with Zidane having announced that the final against Italy would be his last professional game, another U-turn permitting, they now had one last chance to put right a record that did not do justice to two players who in so many ways were perfectly matched.

Team: Barthez, Sagnol, Thuram, Gallas, Abidal, Vieira (56), Makelele, Ribery (100), Zidane, Malouda, Henry (107)
Subs: Diarra (56) Trezeguet (100) Wiltord (107)

It took just 6 minutes for Zidane to stamp his mark on his last ever match. Henry's headed flick-on reached Malouda, who drove into the box before being brought down by Materazzi and the referee pointed to the spot. Zidane stepped up and casually chipped his penalty in off the crossbar, though there was some initial uncertainty over whether the ball had crossed the line.

Italy responded well and were quickly back on level terms when a corner from Pirlo was met by Materazzi, who made up for his penalty indiscretion by thumping a header past France goalkeeper Barthez.

As some had feared, Henry was cutting a rather isolated figure upfront, and he struggled to make any impact in the opening half. But soon after the break, he burst into life with two trademark runs that had the Italian defence back-tracking.

The game became an open affair, with both sides attacking with gusto. Italy came within a whisker of taking the lead when Toni was adjudged offside after heading in a Pirlo free-kick, while at the other end Henry's pace continued to threaten and Buffon had to be alert to parry away his snap-shot.

As the minutes ticked by, France began to gain a foothold but were unable to convert their dominance into a lead. The game entered extra-time and moments later Malouda was presented with a great chance but was denied by a last-ditch Cannavaro tackle. Ribery poked agonisingly wide before being replaced by Trezeguet while a visibly exhausted Henry made way for Wiltord. Soon after, Buffon tipped a header from Zidane over the bar.

It was to be Zidane's final chance to go out in a blaze of glory, but instead he left the stage in disgrace. With 10 minutes left of extra-time, he became embroiled in an off-the-ball dispute with Materazzi and, inexplicably, head-butted the Italian in the chest, who fell to the floor in exaggerated agony.

With the referee unaware of what had happened, the fourth official beckoned him over and informed him. Zidane was duly shown the red card and as he traipsed off the pitch, past the Jules Rimet trophy itself, it was as if someone had ripped up the script for how he would end his career and rewritten it with a barely believable plot twist. How could a player of such elegance be reduced to a moment of unrestrained violence in the biggest football match on earth? Zidane later attributed his actions to what he claimed were deeply personal and offensive comments by Materrazi during their altercation.

His French teammates looked shell-shocked, but they held on to force a penalty shoot-out. Trezeguet missed for France, while Pirlo, Materazzi, Daniele de Rossi, Alessandro del Piero and Grosso converted to give Italy the trophy.

Zidane's moment of infamy, which became as iconic a World Cup image as Pele swapping shirts with Bobby Moore in 1970 or Maradona's Hand of God in 1986, would be dissected for months and years to come, but Henry faced his own, albeit smaller, demons. In less than two months, he had appeared in football's two most prestigious finals, scoring no goals and losing both. No other period in his career had promised so much and delivered so little.

40

Liverpool 1 Arsenal 3
FA Cup Third Round
6 January 2007

The importance of Henry signing a contract extension at the end of the 2005/06 season, immediately after the disappointment of their Champions League final defeat to Barcelona, was intensified by the departure of four of Arsenal's most distinguished players (Cole, Campbell, Pires and Bergkamp) that summer. With Vieira having left the previous year, Arsenal had now lost almost half of the 'Invincibles' team and for their captain and talisman to have also exited the club would have been too much for their fans to take.

Even with Henry staying, many had feared the club were facing a period of transition. The 2006/07 season would see them move into the brand new 60,000-capacity Emirates Stadium, located just down the road from their old home Highbury, and the club had taken on significant debt to finance its construction. It made the task of replacing so many established stars appear doubly challenging.

The stadium move had always been part a long-term strategy for the club, but key to that plan was their continued participation in the Champions League, worth tens of millions of pounds to the club each season. It was something they had almost begun to take for granted in recent years, but they had no god-given right to be in the competition.

Five months into Arsenal's season there had been little to dissuade those who had predicted they may struggle in their debut campaign at their sparkling new address. Despite remaining unbeaten at Emirates stadium in all competitions, five away league defeats by Christmas seemed to have ruled them out of the title race, and after a strong start to their Champions League campaign they had ended up stumbling to qualification.

Not helping matters had been the absence of Henry, who, by the time they faced Liverpool in the third round of the FA Cup, had just returned after missing eight games through injury. The previous summer, Henry had played a key role in France reaching the World Cup final in Germany, where they lost to Italy on penalties. But according to Arsène Wenger, who was speaking ahead of the Liverpool game, his five appearances at the tournament had come at a cost to Arsenal:

> No matter how good you are, if you are not fresh, hungry and completely free in your movement you have no chance. I felt that after the World Cup with France going into the final and then being used in the friendlies, I knew they would hit the wall. I've seen it four times after World Cups with players who have gone far [...] You could tell he was mentally tired, he was not as present in the fight, not as sharp in his runs as before. You don't lose that in a month but you have periods when you go through a little bit of fatigue.

Some went even further than Wenger and questioned whether injuries had taken such a toll on the thirty-year-old that he would never reach his old heights. Others, however, went even further, wondering whether his head had been turned by the overtures of Barcelona the previous summer. Some even suspected he'd made a pact with Arsenal to give them one more season, agreeing to lead them into their new stadium before being granted his dream move. In short, was his mind elsewhere?

In any case, no one connected with Arsenal would have been disappointed to see Henry return from injury ahead of the Liverpool game (his comeback game had been against Charlton at the Emirates four days earlier, scoring a penalty in a 4-0 victory). With the Premiership almost certainly out of reach, the FA Cup offered perhaps their best chance of a trophy, and with Henry in the side their prospects could only be enhanced.

Team: Almunia, Eboue (66), Toure, Senderos, Clichy , Hleb, Flamini, Gilberto, Rosicky, Henry (88), Van Persie (72)
Subs: Hoyte (66), Baptista (72), Walcott (88)

The early moments of the match saw Liverpool enjoy plenty of possession, with Arsenal reduced to counter-attacks. Nevertheless it was the away side that created the first real chance when a smart pass by Van Persie found Rosicky but Liverpool goalkeeper Dudek came out to intercept.

A series of rash challenges briefly threatened to turn the match sour and Liverpool midfielder Alonso was booked for diving after clashing with Gilberto in the Arsenal box. Crouch then had a great chance for Liverpool but ballooned his volley over the bar, and Liverpool were to rue the missed opportunity soon after as Arsenal took the lead.

Arsenal won possession in their own half and Czech midfielder Rosicky swapped passes with Hleb down the right flank. Hleb pulled a low cross back to the edge of the penalty area and Rosicky curled a sumptuous shot over Dudek and into the far side of Liverpool's net.

On the stroke of half-time, Rosicky put Arsenal in a commanding position with his second goal of the match. Henry played a pass inside to Rosicky, who ran at the Liverpool defence, evading a series of challenges before unleashing a fizzing shot from the edge of the box that beat Dudek's outstretched arm and nestled in the corner.

Liverpool responded well in the second half and were putting Arsenal under relentless pressure as they searched for a way back into the game. On 71 minutes, they found one when a corner by former Arsenal player Pennant was headed towards goal and Kuyt diverted it beyond Almunia.

But with 6 minutes left, Arsenal wrapped up victory thanks to a mesmeric goal by Henry. Collecting the ball in the centre circle, he had four Liverpool defenders ahead of him and little by way of support. But Henry showed his uncanny knack of processing a situation in a fraction of a second and coming up with a solution. Aware that Liverpool were playing a high line in their frantic quest to equalise, Henry knocked the ball beyond their defence and gave chase. Despite Carragher having a good 4-yard head-start on Henry, they both arrived at the ball together. But while Henry kept his cool, Carragher panicked and went to ground. The ball came loose and Henry was on it like a flash. He charged towards goal, taking the ball past a retreating Liverpool defender in the box before launching a low shot that beat Dudek.

Henry departed the pitch shortly after his goal to applause from all four stands. He was one of the few players in Premiership history to have elicited such a reaction from opposing fans on more than one occasion (he also received the same treatment from Portsmouth supporters). With questions surrounding his form and fitness (not to mention his future) it was a timely reminder of Henry's enduring talent.

41

Arsenal 2 Manchester United 1
Premier League
21 January 2007

Arsenal's 2006/07 title challenge never did get off the ground and by the time league leaders Manchester United came to visit in January they were already fifteen points off the top of the table. Hopes of completing their debut season at Emirates Stadium with a trophy rested with their continued participation in the Champions League, FA Cup and Carling Cup, though little about their form since August suggested they were likely to lift any of them.

The match with Man United did, however, offer Arsenal an opportunity to give fans an occasion that would make them feel more at home in their new stadium. Victories over Tottenham and Liverpool earlier in the season had already helped with the settling in period, but a win over the Manchester giants would represent their first against a truly elite club.

They went into the game off the back of an impressive 2-0 victory at Blackburn, which featured a sensational goal from Henry to complete the scoring, exchanging passes with Fabregas before launching a brilliant first-time curler into the top corner. It was his third in three games and he seemed now to be over the injuries that had kept him on the sidelines earlier in the season. Nevertheless, questions over his future still persisted.

Team: Lehmann, Eboue (89), Toure, Senderos, Clichy, Hleb (67), Fabregas, Flamini (79), Rosicky, Henry, Adebayor
Subs: Van Persie (67), Baptista (79), Hoyte (89)

In keeping with their position at the top of the table, Man United started the game confidently and both Giggs and Ronaldo were off target with early efforts, and they even had the elements in their favour with a strong tailwind helping them gain the ascendancy.

But slowly Arsenal came in to the match and Henry should have done better than head straight at 'keeper Van der Sar from an Adebayor cross. They were then denied what appeared a clear penalty when Henry was brought down by Neville, but Arsenal's appeals were in vain.

United finished the half the stronger, with Rooney and Larsson both testing Lehmann with headers, and 8 minutes after the break they went in front. Evra surged down the lift and drilled in a cross that reached Rooney at the back post and his diving header found the net.

With 7 minutes left a draw seemed the most Arsenal could hope for, but a remarkable finale was in store. First Van Persie got on the end of a Rosicky cross – unknowingly breaking his metatarsal in the process – to bring Arsenal level, and then with 90 minutes on the clock, Arsenal sealed a dramatic victory with a goal that had the Emirates bouncing with a vigour that hadn't been seen since it opened its doors six months earlier.

Following a one-two with Rosicky, Eboue whipped a cross into the box where Henry had pulled off the 6-yard line and he headed powerfully beyond Van der Sar. He celebrated in familiar fashion, with a deadpan expression planted on his face, but as the crowd settled Adebayor managed to coax a belated dance out of him on the touchline.

The victory meant little to Arsenal in terms of their league ambitions, which were already reduced to finishing in the top four, but as *The Guardian* commented the following day, the result also carried symbolic value: 'All new grounds require folklore to endow them with an identity,' wrote Kevin McCarra. 'Memories have to accrue before fans can feel wholly at home.'

They were not to know it at the time, but the game would also acquire added significance as Henry's final show-stopping moment in an Arsenal shirt – for a few years, anyway.

42

Arsenal 1 PSV Eindhoven 1
(PSV Won 2-1 on Aggregate)
Champions League Knockout Stage
7 March 2007

A 1-0 away defeat in the first leg of their Champions League knockout tie against Dutch club PSV Eindhoven gave Arsenal plenty to do in the return fixture if they were to salvage any remaining hopes of silverware. By the time the second leg came around, they had been eliminated from both domestic cups and morale was low.

Henry's recurrent injury problems had once again reared their head, with a foot complaint meaning he started the second leg on the bench having sat out Arsenal's previous few games. It had been a hugely disappointing season for the Arsenal captain, registering just twelve goals in twenty-six appearances in all competitions – his worst stats since arriving at the club eight years earlier.

Could Henry provide redemption by leading Arsenal to Champions League glory, or were we witnessing the final death rattle of a glorious career in red and white? These were the uncomfortable questions now being asked of a player whose aura of greatness had diminished to a residual sheen.

Team: Lehmann, Toure, Gallas, Gilberto, Clichy (85), Ljungberg (75), Fabregas, Denilson, Hleb, Baptista (66), Adebayor
Subs: Henry (66), Diaby (75), Walcott (85)

Arsenal's early efforts to force an opening were met with resilience by a PSV side that looked determined to hold on to their narrow first-leg lead. The best chance of the early period came from Arsenal's Toure who fired wide from distance, and the Ivorian defender went close again in the 21st minute with another powerful drive that was parried by PSV keeper Gomez.

When the breakthrough came after 58 minutes, it was in fortuitous fashion. Denilson's corner forced an error from Gomez, and the unlucky Alex, on loan from Chelsea, diverted the ball into his own net to level the tie.

Arsenal were suddenly rampant, with Alex making amends for his error with a crucial block from Adebayor. Fabregas then shot over when he should have scored after he was set up by Hleb.

In the second half, Arsenal continued to dominate, although they were fortunate not to concede a penalty when Denilson appeared to barge Farfan to the ground.

On 66 minutes, Arsène Wenger attempted to force home his side's advantage by sending on Henry for Baptista, and the skipper soon tested Gomez with a free kick. However, Arsenal's night was about to take a significant turn for the worse.

Henry was moving around the pitch in a way that no one who had seen him in his pomp could have possibly imaged, looking tentative and utterly bereft of the physical attributes that made him so special. When he pulled up with what appeared to be a groin injury, it was to little surprise, and one was left wondering how a player in his condition could have even made the bench.

If that wasn't bad enough, with 8 minutes left, PSV scored a vital away goal when Medez whipped in a free kick that was met by Alex, who headed home, meaning Arsenal needed to score twice to qualify.

The blow of the late goal left them with nothing left to give and the game petered out with barely a chance created. Arsenal were out of the Champions League and their season was effectively over, save for their annual push for a top-four finish in the league.

Two days later, it was confirmed that Henry would miss the remainder of the campaign because of groin and stomach injuries. Wenger responded to the news by declaring that Henry would be ready for the start of the following season. What he did not know, or perhaps chose not to reveal, was that next season Henry would be a Barcelona player.

It is not on record precisely when the decision over Henry's future was made. Many believe a gentleman's agreement had been struck between the player and Arsenal way back in May 2006, allowing him to leave on the condition that he signed a contract extension and stayed for another season, enabling Arsenal to secure a sizeable transfer fee when he left.

Confirmation eventually arrived in June, five weeks after the end of the English season, that he would be joining Barcelona in a £16-million deal after eight years at Arsenal. Explaining his choice, Henry focussed on the uncertainty over Wenger's future as his main motive for leaving, as well as the departure in May of Arsenal vice-chairman David Dein due to 'irreconcilable differences' with the rest of the board. Dein's close relationship with Henry was common knowledge and his son, Darren, was best man at the Frenchman's wedding.

'Arsène has been part of my life for as long as I can remember,' Henry wrote in *The Sun* newspaper,

> Unfortunately and understandably, he has said that at this moment he will not commit to the club past the expiration of his current deal, which finishes at the end of the coming season. I respect his decision and his honesty but I will be thirty-one at the end of next season and I cannot take the chance to be there without Arsène Wenger and David Dein.

Some reacted with incredulity to his explanation and in later years Henry was more candid in admitting that it was Arsenal's decline and inability to compete for the biggest trophies that forced his decision.

Had Arsenal known he would suffer such injury problems in his final season, they may well have cashed in on him the previous summer when it is thought that there were £50 million bids on the table from both Barcelona and Real Madrid. But without the benefit of such hindsight all they could do was deal with the here and now – and from that viewpoint letting Henry go after 8 years' service seemed like the mutually agreeable decision.

He had arrived a flop and departed a legend. Now a fresh challenge awaited.

43

France 2 Lithuania 0
European Championships Qualifier
17 October 2007

When the draw was made for the 2008 European Championship qualifiers, Henry must have been licking his lips in anticipation. Just five goals away from becoming France's all-time record goalscorer, a series of double headers against international minnows including the Faroe Islands, Georgia and Lithuania presented Henry with the perfect chance to break a record that dated back twenty years to the great Michel Platini.

By the time Henry left Arsenal for Barcelona in June 2007, France had won six of their seven qualifying matches, with Henry having edged two goals closer to Platini's coveted record. Henry went into his debut season at Barcelona with high hopes of a fruitful campaign that would culminate with him appearing in his sixth major international tournament, to be co-hosted by Austria and Switzerland that summer.

As it turned out, nineteen goals for Barça was a more than respectable return, but it somewhat masked what was a difficult start to his time in Spain, which saw a return of the injury problems that blighted his final months at Arsenal. Furthermore, while Zidane's retirement after the 2006 World Cup had seemingly left the path clear for Henry to become France's figurehead, at Barcelona he had the opposite dilemma, too often playing in the shadows of Cameroonian Eto'o and the fast-emerging Argentine Messi. Stranded out on the left wing, often in place of the injured Brazilian Ronaldinho, it was as if Henry had regressed back to his Juventus days, a square peg in a round hole.

'I have never run as much in all my career,' Henry said, as questions were asked over Barcelona's decision to spend £16 million on him. 'Never, never, never, never, never. Instead of running off the shoulder of defenders 30 metres from goal, I'm going from 60! As far as beating the last man is concerned, forget it, my legs are gone by then.' His troubled campaign ended with no trophies: a disaster for the Catalan club, in any season.

In theory, Henry's outings for France should have offered him respite from his Catalan burdens, not least as he was able to play in his preferred position upfront. But his relationship with the French public had become an uneasy one, reaching new depths when he was booed off against Colombia in a friendly. Nevertheless, with Platini's record in clear sight, he needed no motivating as France entered the business end of their qualifying campaign.

His teammates, in contrast, seemed to have begun resting on their laurels, judging by a shock 1-0 home defeat to Scotland that suddenly put France's qualification hopes in serious doubt. Fortunately, their next match saw them travel to the lowly Faroe Islands, where a 6-0 victory went some way to putting France back on track, as well as nudging Henry equal with Platini on forty-one goals.

Team: Landreau, Thuram, Gallas, Abidal, Ribery, Toulalan, Makelele, Diarra (69), Malouda, Henry, Benzema
Subs: Ben Arfa (69)

France knew that victory over Lithuania at the Stade de la Beaujoire in Nantes would allow them to climb above Scotland into second place in the group behind Italy, and leave them just one win away from confirming their qualification.

Almost from the first whistle they peppered the Lithuanian goal, with Ribery threatening in the first minute with a powerful shot that Lithuanian goalkeeper Karčemarskas tipped against the crossbar. Henry's gifted young strike-partner Benzema then had an effort deflected just wide and Malouda also struck the woodwork as France did everything but score.

Gallas, Malouda, Henry and Benzema all passed up further opportunities to put France in front before half-time and the second period continued in familiar fashion, with Henry firing over and then being denied twice by Karčemarskas. The pressure was relentless and in the 80th minute France finally found a way through with an historic goal.

Ben Arfa was the instigator, supplying a left-wing cross that was deflected into the path of Henry, who made no mistake from close range to give France the lead and become his country's greatest ever goalscorer. Within 60 seconds, Henry had added another to his record total, racing on to Toulalan's through ball and calmly side-footing home.

There was a neat symmetry to Henry's achievement; twenty years to the month of his international debut, he had overtaken a record that had stood for – you guessed it – twenty years.

Henry may have become a scapegoat among fans who were disappointed that France had failed to build on their successes of 1998 and 2002, but his name had now been etched that bit deeper into the annuls of French football history.

44

Real Madrid 2 Barcelona 6
La Liga, 2 May 2009

In the Spring of 2008, Henry gave a heartfelt interview to the BBC's *Football Focus* programme, in which he responded to questions over his performances since joining Barcelona the previous summer:

> They signed the guy from Arsenal, so they want to see the guy from Arsenal. I'm trying to explain to some people sometimes, 'Don't expect the Henry from Arsenal' – it's not the same thing! If you ask any kind of forward to play on the wing, he will do his best. But will he be as efficient as he can be as a centre forward? I don't think so.

With nineteen goals in all competitions making him Barcelona's top scorer, Henry's first season in Catalunya was far from an unmitigated failure, but it had clearly not gone entirely to plan either. The injuries that had hindered him for well over a year continued to cause him trouble, and when he did play it was out on the left, a position that frustrated him, not least because it came with added defensive duties.

Coach Frank Rijkaard's favoured 4-3-3 formation meant there was only one central striker's berth and that invariably went to the exuberant Cameroonian Eto'o. Meanwhile, the development of the young Argentina Messi into a player many now believed would join the ranks of Pelé and Maradona as the greatest ever also took some of the spotlight away from Henry, who at Arsenal had got used to enjoying it all to himself.

His problems were even the subject of forensic scrutiny in a BBC online article, in which former England striker turned television presenter Gary Lineker, who also found himself exiled to the wing during a spell at Barcelona in the 1990s, suggested that Henry had struggled with the transition from being a big fish in a small pond to the very opposite.

I'm a lot different to Henry. He is a much better player than I was. But he was always the fulcrum of Arsenal's play. He's not at Barça. He used to be a winger when he was younger and it's not a difficult position compared to where he was playing but it's probably not giving him as much satisfaction or involvement.

Coach Rijkaard, who was clinging on to his job in the face of fierce criticism, also jumped to Henry's defence:

Thierry has suffered with the aftermath of an injury and for so long that has stopped him from performing optimally. But he's had his value in many games. He hasn't quite been the player we imagined when we bought him but he is a player who I still think can become that.

Former Barcelona vice-president Sandro Rosell was not so compassionate. 'Whoever signed him deserves a clip round the ear,' he had said in December. 'He should have been given an exhaustive medical.'

To say that Henry was used as a scapegoat would perhaps be overstating it, but had Barcelona not ended the 2007/08 season trophyless – the second campaign in a row they had done so – it is likely that the criticism of him would have been far less severe. This was a club that demanded trophies, and it was to no-one's surprise that coach Rijkaard was replaced that summer. The pressure to avoid a third barren season was immense.

Fast forward seven months and, under new coach Pep Guardiola, Barcelona had well and truly risen to the challenge. As they entered 2009 they looked to be cruising towards the La Liga title and were even in contention for an unprecedented sextuple of trophies.

With his injury problems behind him, Henry, with twenty-six goals, was key to Barcelona's resurgence and, having been written off by many, was now showing there was plenty of life left in his thirty-two-year-old legs. He was helped by a tactical tweak by Guardiola that saw Messi drop deeper into a 'false nine' position, with Henry and Eto'o moving forward into more conventional centre-forward roles. Back on more familiar territory, Henry flourished.

However, just as it looked like his first trophy in Spain was a formality, two straight league defeats reopened the door to challengers. With their once unassailable lead over fierce rivals Real Madrid now cut to just four points with five games remaining, Barcelona travelled to the Spanish capital for a crunch league match that would go some way to deciding the destiny of the title.

Team: Valdes, Alves, Pique, Puyol, Abidal, Xavi, Toure (85), Inieste (85), Messi, Eto'o, Henry (60)

Subs: Keita (60), Busquets (85), Bojan (85)

The deep-rooted political acrimony that lies at the heart of the rivalry between Barcelona and Real Madrid, allied with their long-running shared dominance of Spanish football, makes every game between them a veritable powder-keg. Never was this more true than at Real Madrid's Bernabeu stadium, for what had been rightfully hyped as one of the most eagerly anticipated encounters in the history of the match known as *El Clásico*.

While Barcelona's four-point cushion at the top of the table meant they could afford to drop points, reigning champions Real Madrid knew only a victory would realistically keep them in contention for a third straight title, and they got off to the perfect start.

Defender Ramos ghosted past Barcelona's left-back Abidal on the right and crossed for an unmarked Higuain to head powerfully beyond goalkeeper Valdes. But Barca were back on terms almost immediately and it was Henry with the goal, latching on to Messi's pass and caressing the ball beyond Real goalkeeper Casillas.

A pulsating, end-to-end spectacle was unfolding and Real nearly hit back as Higuain zipped the ball across the face of goal and Alves almost diverted it into his own net. But the rest of the half belonged to Barca as they produced an attacking masterclass.

After Henry was fouled by Cannavaro on the left, Xavi's free-kick picked out Puyol to score with a bullet header. Barcelona were now dominating the midfield and only two smart saves from Casillas prevented them extending their lead.

But with 36 minutes gone, Real's resolve was broken when Xavi robbed Diarra of possession and sent Messi haring through on goal. He approached Casillas and nudged a delicious shot with the outside of his foot that nestled in the corner.

Trailing 3-1 at half-time, Real knew they had nothing to lose and came out from the break with all guns blazing. But after Ramos had pulled a goal back with a neat header, Barca simply upped the gears and restored their advantage. Xavi picked out Henry with a whipped pass, and as Casillas charged out of his box, the Frenchman reached the ball fractionally ahead of him and passed the ball around his flailing limbs and watched it trickle into the net.

Two more goals followed as a resounding victory became a humiliating trouncing, first through Messi again who collected yet another fine pass by Xavi to finish with aplomb and then defender Pique with his first ever league goal for Barca, shooting home from a narrow angle at the second attempt.

The final whistle went, putting a merciful end to Real's misery. Barça had all-but secured their 19th Spanish title – which they would wrap up a couple of weeks later – and Henry had played his greatest and most memorable match for the club.

But La Liga was by no means the start and end of Barça's trophy-winning ambitions for the season. Victory in the Copa del Rey soon followed, but at the top of their wish-list was the holy grail of European football, the Champions League, until now conspicuous by its absence on Henry's lavish honours list.

45

Barcelona 2 Manchester United 0
Champions League Final
27 May 2009

With the Spanish league title and Copa del Rey both already won, and a place in the Champions League final secured, Pep Guardiola's debut season as Barcelona coach had already exceeded all expectations. Not only were the trophies raining in, but the style of football he had cultivated had some observers asking if this was the best club side ever.

As for Henry, all doubts about him still being able to perform at the highest level had been well and truly laid to rest. In coach Pep Guardiola's finely tuned system, he formed a front three with Eto'o and Messi that over the course of the season became the most prolific in Spanish league history, their seventy-two goals surpassing the sixty-six scored by Real Madrid's Puskas, Di-Stéfano and Del Sol in 1960/61.

Now all that stood between Henry and Barcelona completing an historic treble were Champions League holders Manchester United, who were bidding to become the first team to retain the title since AC Milan in 1990. For their part, Barca were hoping to win the trophy for the second time in four years – the last occasion being their 2-1 victory over Henry's Arsenal in Paris in 2006.

The final against Man United, to be played at the Stadio Olimpico in Rome, gave Henry the chance to exercise several demons that had arisen in Paris three years earlier. During that match, Henry had missed three gilt-edged chances, including a one-on-one to put Arsenal 3-1 up with 20 minutes remaining. To compound matters, the game would go down as one of eight major finals he played throughout his career in which he failed to score (his single goal in a final came in France's Confederations Cup victory in 2003) – a statistic that caused many to conclude that he wasn't a 'big game' player. Furthermore, while he had won almost everything as a player, the Paris defeat meant that the Champions League still eluded him.

While attention ahead of the 2009 final focussed on Barcelona's record-shattering season, those who had keenly observed Henry's career were aware that for the Frenchman this match was loaded with cathartic potential.

Team: Valdés, Puyol, Touré, Piqué, Sylvinho, Busquets, Xavi, Iniesta (90+2), Messi, Henry (72), Eto'o
Subs: Keita (72), Pedro (90+2)

Barcelona had only reached the final by the skin of their teeth thanks to a dramatic, last-gasp goal from Iniesta in their semi-final second leg against Chelsea at Stamford Bridge – a game that Henry missed due to a ligament injury that had left him a doubt for the remainder of the season. With defenders Abidal, Alves and Marquez all ruled out through a combination of suspension and injury and Iniesta doubtful too, Barcelona needed to ensure they were firing on all cylinders upfront.

Luckily for Barça, Henry recovered in time and was named in the line-up as part of the triumvirate that had demolished everything in its wake for the previous nine months.

Despite going into the game as favourites, Barcelona found themselves penned back in the opening period with Ronaldo going close on three occasions for Man United. But with their first meaningful attack, Barcelona took the lead.

Cameroon striker Eto'o neatly turned past Vidic in the box before toe-poking a powerful shot that goalkeeper Van der Sar got his hand to but could not prevent ricocheting into the net.

The goal gave Barcelona a visible injection of confidence, allowing Messi to pull the strings up front and Xavi and Iniesta to take control of midfield. Alex Ferguson responded at half-time by replacing Anderson with Tevez and moving Rooney into a more central position, but the change did little to quell Barcelona's dominance. Soon after the break, Henry tricked his way past Ferdinand only to be denied by the legs of Van der Sar.

Xavi almost doubled Barcelona's lead with a 20-yard free-kick following Vidic's foul on Messi and Man United were showing little sign of a response. With 25 minutes remaining, they played their final card by bringing on Berbatov for Park, but 5 minutes later Barcelona deservedly scored a second.

Xavi was the creator with a cross that looked too high for Messi, but he belied his size by leaping expertly to send a header back from whence it came and Van der Sar could only look on helplessly as the ball floated over him and into the corner of the net.

United looked to mount an instant response, with Valdes blocking from Ronaldo, but there was no way back and Barcelona had rounded off a dream season by adding the Champions League to their La Liga Spanish Cup victories.

Henry finally got his hands on the trophy that had evaded his grasp for so long, and he savoured the moment, lifting it high above his head and taking in the adulation of the crowd.

'This is incredible,' Henry said after the game.

I had wanted to win the Champions League for a long time. It's something that I was missing. It's a special feeling because to win a treble in modern football is not easy and yet we have done it. No Spanish team has achieved what we have, to win a treble, and I think everyone will remember this Barça side. I'm delighted because I always wanted to make history at this club and we've done just that.

But Barcelona were not finished there. By December 2009, they had added the FIFA World Club Cup, the UEFA Super Cup and the Spanish Super Cup to their roll-call, becoming the first club side ever to win six trophies in a calendar year.

Henry's record of goalless finals persisted, but his contribution across the season could not be denied by even his harshest critic. Having become an Invincible at Arsenal, he was now part of the immortals of Barcelona's greatest ever epoch.

46

France 1 Republic of Ireland 1
(France Won 2-1 on Aggregate)
World Cup Qualifying Play-Off 2nd Leg
18 November 2009

Despite France's disastrous showing at Euro 20008, where they finished bottom of their group, coach Raymond Domenech clung onto his job to lead Les Bleus into their 2010 World Cup qualifying campaign, which would they hoped would lead them to South Africa, the first time the showpiece tournament was to be held on the African continent.

Those convinced that Domenech was incapable of turning France's fortunes around were given more grist to their mill when they lost their opening qualifier 3-1 away to Austria in early September 2008, but in their next match at home to Serbia a goal apiece from Henry and Anelka seemed to have put them back on track.

The first half of France's qualifying campaign ran simultaneously with Henry's momentous season with Barcelona, which saw him score twenty-six goals as the Catalan club swept up every trophy on offer.

But the following season, Henry struggled to recapture the same form and his position in the side came under increasing threat from the young Spanish striker Pedro. Henry had to wait almost three months to score his first goal of the season in a 4-2 victory at home to Mallorca, and questions over the thirty-two-year-old's durability as a top-level player began to rear their head once again.

Seven days after his goal against Mallorca, he was back on international duty, captaining France in circumstances they could well have avoided. Despite facing substantially weaker nations in their qualifying group, they could only finish second, meaning they faced a two-legged play-off to reach the finals that summer. The draw pitched France together with the Republic of Ireland.

The first leg at Croke Park Stadium in Dublin was a one-sided affair, with a late strike from Anelka the least France deserved, giving France a narrow victory but crucially an 'away' goal that would count double in the event of the aggregate score remaining level.

It meant that France could prepare for the second leg four days later in Paris with an air of calm professionalism, knowing they had one foot on the plane to South Africa and now only had to complete the job.

Team: Lloris, Sagna, Gallas, Escude (9), Evra, L. Diarra, A. Diarra, Gourcuff (88), Anelka, Gignac (57), Henry
Subs: Squillaci (9), Govou (57), Malouda (88)

With France seeming content to sit on their aggregate lead, Ireland began to impose themselves on the match, and after 32 minutes took a well-earned lead. Kilbane played a neat ball through to Duff on the left and he chased to the byline to pull it back for Keane, who side-footed beyond the dive of goalkeeper Lloris from 10 yards to bring the tie level.

Suddenly, the Irish dream was on and half-time arrived with goalkeeper Given so far untroubled. They started the second half with their tails up and a chance soon fell the way of defender O'Shea, who shot rashly over from a tight angle. A second goal for Ireland would have left the French needing a daunting two to qualify.

France surged forward late in the game, trying to grab the goal that would avert the need for extra-time, but that would have been cruel on the Irish, who deservedly remained on terms at the end of the 90 minutes.

The home side felt they should have had a penalty in the first period of extra-time when Anelka went through and fell as keeper Given came out, but the referee pointed for a goal kick. If that was controversial, it paled into insignificance compared with what followed.

With 13 minutes of extra-time gone, a free-kick from inside the French half was lofted into the Ireland penalty area. It broke to Henry, who controlled the ball and flicked it across the face of goal for Gallas to head into the net from point-blank range. Gallas wheeled away in celebration and Henry quickly followed. But back in the penalty area, the Ireland players were furious and chased after the referee.

Television replays soon confirmed the cause of their protestations. Henry had clearly – and seemingly deliberately – handled the ball twice to bring it under control before passing for Gallas to score. To compound Ireland's anger, two France players appeared to be offside when the original free-kick was taken.

After the game, Henry admitted to the handball, but stopped short of apologising or admitting it had been intentional.

> I will be honest, it was a handball. But I'm not the ref. I played it, the ref
> allowed it. That's a question you should ask him. The ball ran up against
> my hand and I continued to play. The referee did not blow his whistle and
> there was a goal. I would have preferred that it happened differently but
> this is not down to me – it is the referee.

The reaction was explosive. Before long, the first calls for the game to be
replayed were aired (FIFA soon ruled this out), with Ireland's assistant
manager Liam Brady saying it was essential 'for the dignity and integrity of
football'. Soon enough, high-level Irish government officials had joined in
the same chorus.

Criticism of Henry quickly escalated beyond the handball itself, with
his very character and moral fibre placed on public trial. Many claimed
that by celebrating the goal he had shown a brazen lack of contrition.
Others condemned him as 'conceited' and 'two-faced' for sitting on the
turf consoling the distraught Irish defender Dunne on the pitch at the final
whistle, akin to offering comfort to a cuckolded man whose wife he had
cheated with.

Cheated. A word that few would have associated with Henry before that
night in Paris, but that he would now carry with him for the rest of his career.

For a couple of days, Henry remained silent, but then resurfaced to issue
a statement:

> I have said at the time and I will say again that, yes, I handled the ball. I
> am not a cheat and never have been. As a footballer you do not have the
> beauty of the television to slow the pace of the ball down 100 times to be
> able to make a conscious decision.
>
> People are viewing a slow-motion version of what happened and not
> what I or any other footballer faces in the game. If people look at it in full
> speed you will see that it was an instinctive reaction. It is impossible to be
> anything other than that. I have never denied that the ball was controlled
> with my hand. I told the Irish players, the referee and the media this after
> the game.
>
> Naturally I feel embarrassed at the way that we won and feel extremely
> sorry for the Irish, who definitely deserve to be in South Africa. Of course
> the fairest solution would be to replay the game, but it is not in my control.

Henry's words did little to quell the storm, eagerly whipped up by a media
who knew this was a story that would run and run. With no shortage of
rent-a-quotes keen to vilify Henry, only those inside the game seemed
willing to defend him, perhaps aware more than most that such chicanery is
routine practice in football.

He was, in a sense, a victim of context. The hopes and dreams of a small nation cruelly snatched away by an opponent big and ugly enough to win clean. It was like David being slain by a Goliath pumped full of steroids. The narrative was simply too emotionally charged to just fizzle out.

One man to step forward as a character witness was his former coach Arsène Wenger, who felt strongly that France should offer a replay, 'for the credibility of France going to the World Cup', but also to ensure that Henry was not left hung out to dry:

> Now let's be realistic. Football, and sport in general, is full of heroes who have cheated 10 times more than Thierry. For me people who bought referees, who took drugs, they are the real cheats in sport. Thierry Henry has fourteen years behind of fair behaviour in sport and he is singled out today, for me, in the wrong way. You mustn't go overboard with Thierry's behaviour. He made one mistake, and who hasn't made mistakes in life?
>
> Thierry's was an instinctive reaction of a striker. When the ball goes too far, you take your hand and use it. He meant to do it but what I mean is it is a reaction of a player when the ball is going out to keep it in.

Wenger was correct to highlight Henry's unblemished career until this point. He may have cheated – and perhaps would do so again – but he was certainly not the kind of habitual con-artist for whom such behaviour seemed second nature. On the contrary, Henry never relished football's dark arts, far more keen to get on the ball and entertain, thrill, surprise.

Step away from the melodrama and the conclusion one may draw is far more prosaic. As their captain, Henry, who had never quite been taken to the hearts of the French public, was under huge pressure to lead France to the finals. What is likely is that the intensity of the situation triggered an almost visceral, Darwinian response. The handball, therefore, can be viewed not as evidence of a Machiavellian streak, but of Henry's tunnel-vision determination to fight for World Cup survival. Just as at times in his career he was criticised for playing with a certain insouciance, on this occasion the burden of responsibility lead to him doing something entirely out of character: to cheat.

The fall-out from the Ireland match took its toll on Henry, who later admitted he had considered quitting international football. But like a bank robber returning for 'one last job', Henry could not resist the temptation of a World Cup hurrah in South Africa.

France 1 South Africa 2
World Cup Group Match
22 June 2010

Henry finished the 2009/10 season with his second Spanish league title winner's medal, but it could not mask the fact that he had become no more than a bit-part player at Barcelona. Regularly playing second fiddle to the emerging Spanish talent Pedro, he managed only 21 appearances and four goals all season.

Having been a consistent starter for France during their 2010 World Cup qualifying campaign (in which he finished their joint top scorer with four goals), the weeks before the South Africa tournament saw him phased out of the starting line up as Les Bleus played a series of friendlies in preparation for the finals. With Henry demoted to the bench, coach Raymond Domenech handed the captaincy to left back Evra.

Whether the storm surrounding Henry's handball against the Republic of Ireland that lead to France qualifying for the tournament contributed to Henry losing his place in the side, or if it was simply felt that he was no longer worthy of a starting spot, remains unknown. Certainly, the fact that one of the men to replace him, the Lyon striker Sydney Givou, had managed just two goals all season in Ligue 1, suggested there was more at play then met the eye. More likely is that Henry's displacement was part of an attempt by Domenech – a widely unpopular coach who was rumoured to have a fraught relationship with several of the French squad – to freshen things up.

If that was his idea, it failed miserably as France gathered just a single point from their opening two matches of the tournament, leaving them on the brink of elimination. Henry, who became the first Frenchman to appear in four World Cups, had featured for just 18 minutes over the two games, entering as a late substitute in France's opening fixture, a 0-0 draw with Uruguay. Their next match, a 2-0 defeat to Mexico, was the catalyst for a full-scale French implosion.

At half-time, with the score 0-0, France striker Anelka was said to have launched a foul-mouthed attack on Domenech in response to the coach criticising his first-half performance. Two days later, the French Football Federation sent Anelka home in disgrace for his actions.

Just when Domenech needed his players to rally round, they did the very opposite, responding to Anelka's banishment by refusing to train ahead of their must-win match with South Africa. The shambolic situation escalated when Domenech himself emerged to face the media and read out a statement confirming the players' decision to down tools:

> All the players of the équipe de France, without exception, state their opposition to the decision taken by the FFP to exclude Anelka solely on the basis of facts reported by the press. Consequently, and to mark their opposition to the attitude of the highest authorities [they have decided] not to take part in the session programmed for today.

Arriving in South Africa with a coach who many were amazed was still in his job, and a squad bereft of a Zidane-type figurehead to inspire them to victory (and the only real candidate for that mantle consigned to the bench), expectations for what France could achieve were modest even before the tournament began. But no one could have predicted a squad of seasoned professionals would allow a World Cup campaign, the sport's most prestigious stage, to degenerate into such collective farce. As they prepared to face South Africa, whether or not France stayed in the tournament did not even feel important anymore.

Team: Lloris, Sagna, Gallas, Squillaci, Clichy, Gourcuff, Diarra (82), Diaby, Ribery, Cisse (55), Gignac (46)
Subs: Malouda (46), Henry (55), Govou (82)

With Anelka's shock exclusion and rumours of rifts between players dominating the pre-match talk, it had almost been forgotten that France could still qualify for the knockout rounds, although their chances were slim.

Their task was to secure victory against South Africa in their final group game at the Free State Stadium in Bloemfontein and hope that the result of Mexico's match with Uruguay went their way. South Africa, meanwhile, were striving to avoid becoming the first host nation to fail to progress beyond the group stage of the tournament.

Speculation that the disharmony in the squad would lead to some French players refusing to play in the match did not materialise, although as part of the fall-out from the Anelka debacle, captain Evra was dropped and the armband given to Diarra.

With France playing like a team devoid of spirit or inspiration, South Africa deservedly went ahead after 20 minutes when France goalkeeper Lloris completely missed a corner and Khumalo launched himself at the ball, turning it in off his shoulder.

France's woes took a further turn for the worse 6 minutes later when Gourcuff was sent off for an aerial challenge on Sibaya, and their hopes of qualification were soon reduced to virtually zero when Les Masilela turned the ball back across goal for Mphela to bundle it home at the back post to put South Africa 2-0 up.

Ten minutes after half-time, the substitutes board went up and Henry trotted on to earn his 123rd cap, becoming the first Frenchman to appear in four World Cup finals. The departing Diarra handed Henry his captain's armband and France were left to hope it would have the same kind of transformative effect as Clark Kent donning a cape.

While France needed something approaching a miracle, South Africa required just two more goals to reach the last sixteen, but as their efforts became more frantic, Les Bleus capitalised by snatching one back when Ribery squared for Malouda to tap home.

South Africa continued to come forward but to no avail. The final whistle went and while South Africa were able depart the pitch with their heads held high, France could only bow theirs in shame.

It did not take long for the postmortem to begin. Back in France, Henry was summoned (or went of his own accord, depending on who you believe) for a meeting with France President Nicolas Sarkozy at the Elysée Palace in Paris to provide his version of events. The content of their discussion was never revealed, but publicly Henry was quick to jump to his own defence against accusations that as a senior figure he should have done more to keep the peace.

'I could have been the older brother but I wasn't anymore,' Henry told French TV station Canal+. 'I felt isolated, it doesn't matter who by. They didn't talk to me as they used to. Before they talked to me more. But when you don't have credibility in a group any more it becomes difficult.'

Speaking in New York, three weeks after France's defeat to South Africa, Henry announced that he had played his last game for France. His decision came as no surprise, nor indeed did the sacking of Domenechm, who was replaced by a graduate of the 1998 World Cup winning team, the former defender Laurent Blanc.

'South Africa didn't play any part in it,' Henry insisted. 'I could have announced it before the World Cup but I just didn't want to put that type of cloud on top of the team. My decision was already taken before the World Cup. I think it was time for me to stop after the World Cup.'

It may have ended on the sourest of notes, but Henry's French career had been unparalleled in its distinction. Now the boy from the humble Paris suburb who became France's greatest ever goalscorer was heading for a fresh adventure, far away from Highbury, Camp Nou or the Stade de France.

48

NY Red Bulls 2 Houston Dynamo 2
Major League Soccer
31 July 2010

In mid-July 2010, two days before he confirmed his international retirement, it was announced that Henry would be joining American Major League Soccer club New York Red Bulls from Barcelona on a 'multi-year contract'.

Aged thirty-two, he was certainly still young enough to play in one of Europe's top leagues, but having found himself falling down the pecking order at Camp Nou, he had decided it was the right time to move on.

The 2010 World Cup in South Africa had been an unmitigated disaster for France, and while Henry had only made it onto the pitch for 35 minutes across their three dismal group matches, as one of France's most senior players he received widespread criticism for not doing more to quell the disharmony that engulfed the squad and led to striker Anelka being sent home. Together with his fading role at Barça, the chance to escape the spotlight of Europe made good sense.

Another key factor was that Henry had acquired a strong affection for New York, having been a regular visitor over the years, even befriending illustrious natives such as the film director Spike Lee. The chance to lay down roots in the iconic metropolis while prolonging his playing career was an enticing one.

'It is home in a lot of ways but it is more than that. I have seen a lot of places, and for me, it is the best city in the world,' he would tell *The New York Times* newspaper in an interview in 2012.

After David Beckham, who had joined LA Galaxy in 2007, Henry was the most high-profile European-based player to have made the move to the MLS. Though the sport had experienced false dawns in the United States before, soccer appeared to be on an upward popularity curve and many hoped that Henry's arrival would provide it with an additional push in the right direction.

'This marks an exciting new chapter in my career and life,' Henry said after joining.

It is an honour to play for the New York Red Bulls. I am fully aware of the team's history and my sole goal during my time here is to help win the club its first championship. Knowing Red Bull's significant commitment to soccer locally and internationally, I am confident that my teammates and I will succeed.

Henry made his first Red Bulls appearance against familiar opponents – his old rivals from his Arsenal days, Tottenham Hotspur – in a friendly, scoring the opening goal with a smart finish before the English club came back to win 2-1.

His competitive debut arrived nine days later against Houston Dynamo, at the Robertson Stadium in Houston, as Henry embarked on what most assumed would be the twilight adventure of an extraordinary career.

Team: Coundoul, Albright, Mendes, Miller, Ream, Lindpere, Tchani, Stammle, Kandji, Angel, Henry
Subs: Richards (46) Robinson (90)

Ten minutes was all it took for Henry to make an impact as a Red Bulls player, combining with strike-partner Angel to give the away side the lead. Gathering the ball with his back to goal near the left corner flag, the Frenchman expertly turned his marker before dinking a left-footed cross into the box, which Angel controlled and shot left-footed past goalkeeper Hall.

Houston levelled the score in the 24th minute after Red Bulls defender Mendes slid in on Ngwenya and the referee pointed to the spot. Davis stepped up and converted the kick, tucking the ball low into the right-hand corner of the goal.

Henry nearly restored the Red Bulls' lead in the 30th minute after Kandji fired a low cross into the box that Henry redirected towards goal. Hall went down to push it away, but Angel regained possession and again found Henry who failed to convert.

In a wide open first half, Houston earned their second penalty kick when Ream clipped Ching in the box, but this time Davis rifled his shot over the crossbar.

At the other end, Henry had a golden opportunity to open his account, latching onto an Angel flick-on and bearing down on goal, only to slide his shot fractionally past the post. Just before half-time, Houston were reduced to ten men when Palmer's late challenge on Mendes was punished with a red card.

Both teams threatened to score soon after the break, with Houston's Cruz shooting past the right post and Henry forcing Hall into a save. Then, with half an hour to play, Henry turned provider again, playing in Angel, who took a touch before launching a rocket into the back of the net to put the Red Bulls back in front.

But with 90 minutes on the clock, Henry was denied a victorious debut when Hainault crossed for Houston and Mullan leaped above his marker to score with a fine equalising header.

The Red Bulls had to settle for a solitary point, but amid the disappointment was evidence that everything they had heard from across the pond about their new signing was true. Even if he lacked the explosive pace of yesteryear, he had shown more than enough to hint at exciting times ahead.

Some were drawn to ask why Henry would retreat to a (relatively speaking) footballing backwater like America when he still had so much to offer. But after the traumas of Dublin and South Africa, and the incessant exposure that came with playing for Barcelona, few could have begrudged him his next move being a lifestyle choice rather than a footballing one.

In New York, perhaps for the first time since those halcyon days at Arsenal, where he was worshipped at Highbury but could enjoy a degree of solitude away from the game, Henry could achieve happiness and serenity both on and off the pitch.

49

Arsenal 1 Leeds United 0
FA Cup Third Round
9 January 2012

In December 2011, during the off-season for his MLS club the New York Red Bulls, Henry attended a ceremony at Emirates Stadium for the unveiling of three bronze statues to commemorate a trio of club legends. The recipients were the club's late manager Herbert Chapman, former defensive stalwart Tony Adams and Henry himself.

Henry's own sculpture depicted his famous celebration after scoring a wonder goal against Tottenham at Highbury in November 2002 – a moment that encapsulated how the club had become a part of his very DNA.

Speaking in front of a large crowd that included his former manager Arsène Wenger and Arsenal Chairman Peter Hill-Wood, Henry talked with emotion about the pride he felt at receiving such a permanent memorial to his Arsenal career:

I never thought in my wildest dreams that I would have a statue like this in front of the stadium of the team I love and support. The way the statue is gives the perfect example of the love I have for the club – me kneeling facing the Emirates Stadium and Highbury behind is amazing.

I know some of the press used to kill me for not showing emotion – well, there you go, I am showing emotion for the club I love. Whatever I do, I do it with my heart, that is the way I am. It was not always easy to cope with the pressure of delivering, but from the bottom of my heart, I want to thank Arsenal Football Club for giving me this opportunity to be here in front of this club I love – once a Gooner, always a Gooner.

Rumours had been circulating for weeks that Henry's lasting attachment to Arsenal could yet be formalised beyond his credentials as a fully fledged

'Gooner'. Aged thirty-four, he had been training with the club from November, keeping himself in shape before the MLS season resumed in March.

During those training sessions, Wenger was said to have been surprised by Henry's sharpness given his age. Despite lacking the prestige of the major European leagues, Henry had still recorded impressive stats in the previous MLS season, scoring fourteen goals in twenty-six games and being named in both the MLS Best XI and All-Star lists.

Certainly, assessing Arsenal's options upfront, the idea of Henry returning made good sense. They were far from blessed in this regard (two of their strikers, Chamakh and Gervinho, were about to depart for the African Nations Cup) and after struggling for consistency all campaign, looked to be facing a battle to qualify for the Champions League through their league position. If nothing else, Henry's return would generate excitement among fans who had become somewhat disillusioned with their team's perennial battle for fourth place.

Since leaving Arsenal, he had returned to play at the Emirates just once, coming on as a late substitute for Barcelona in an emotionally charged Champions League match in 2010 that finished 2-2. The reception he received that night, as he warmed up and then during the 17 minutes he soberly wandered around the pitch in an apparent state of self-flagellation (his first touches of the ball were amusingly met with pantomime boos), seemed to reinforce Henry's attachment to the red and white shirt. Perhaps it was on that night he knew his love affair with the club had not quite run its course.

On 6 January, Arsenal finally announced their record goalscorer had rejoined them on a short-term loan that would expire on 17 February, ahead of the resumption of the MLS season. Henry was quick to play down the move, insisting he did not expect to play anything more than a bit-part role in the eight matches for which he would be available:

> I am not coming here to be a hero or prove anything. I am just coming here to help. People have to understand that. I'll be on the bench most of the time – if I can make the bench, that is.
>
> I want to send a message to the fans of New York Red Bulls as well. I always said I would not play in Europe again. But it is hard for me when it comes to Arsenal. I am not coming here for the whole season, I will be back and I want to win the MLS Cup with the Red Bulls. I hope it is a win-win situation where I can help Arsenal and come back fit for the MLS season.

Henry also warned Arsenal fans not to expect the same player that ran English defences riot for eight unforgettable years.

I am not twenty-five anymore. I am not going to take the ball from the middle of the park and dribble past five or six players. I remember Dennis [Bergkamp] and he used to be the main front guy. Suddenly he was playing behind the striker and if you have the awareness to see things before other players, you can get away with not having your legs.

If you look at Ryan Giggs, it's not the same Ryan Giggs who used to take the ball from the wing or from Denis Irwin and dribble past everyone and deliver a great cross. But what Ryan Giggs has is that he can see the game, he is always available, he puts himself in a position where he can receive the ball alone – then you will never lose your touch. That's what I am going to try to bring to this team if I ever have to play.

For all of Henry's attempts to temper expectations, the anticipation ahead of his first game back – a Monday night FA Cup third-round tie against Leeds United at the Emirates – was palpable. More than 1,500 days had passed since his last Arsenal appearance, but the memories of his time at the club were still etched in the minds of the 60,000 fans who descended on the Emirates for an occasion they could not have expected to witness in their wildest dreams.

Team: Szczesny, Coquelin (33), Kosceilny, Squillaci, Miguel, Oxlade-Chamberlain (68), Ramsey, Arteta, Song, Arshavin, Chamakh (68)
Subs: Yennaris (33), Walcott (68), Henry (68)

Henry's mere presence was enough to enliven Emirates Stadium, and when he came out to warm up before the match he received the kind of rapturous reception befitting a player who had earned legendary status at the club.

The physical changes in Henry were striking, looking heavier set and sporting a well-styled beard, amplifying the sense of time that had passed since he last graced the Emirates turf back in 2007. What remained to be seen was the effect that time had borne on Henry the footballer.

The opening half was dominated by the home side, but for all their possession they failed to force a goal. After the break the momentum remained with Arsenal, as Lonergan saved well from Arteta and Arshavin fired across the face of goal.

Henry's increasingly energetic sprinting along the touchline drew a loud reaction from the Arsenal fans, and he was finally introduced with 22 minutes left, replacing Chamakh. He received a hero's welcome as he set about the business of attempting to break down a stubborn Leeds side.

It took him just 10 minutes to remind Arsenal fans, and English football, what they had been missing. When Cameroonian midfielder Song picked up the ball 35 yards from goal, Henry was loitering out on the left wing. With a perfect view across Leeds' backline, Henry made his move and Song played an inch-perfect ball behind the Leeds right back. Just as he had done hundreds of time before in his career, Henry controlled the pass and in the next stride opened out his body and stroked the ball across the goalkeeper and into the far corner. It was the most 'Henry-esque' of goals and it sent the crowd into raptures.

Henry bounded along the touchline in celebration, with arms outstretched, palms open and his eyes bulging with emotion. Reaching Arsène Wenger in the Arsenal dugout, he embraced his coach before beating his chest in a show of uncontrolled fervour. It was one of those all-too-rare moments that reminded you how sport could, on occasion, conjure human drama like nothing else on earth.

Leeds refused to be distracted by the euphoria and almost snatched a replay in the closing stages as Szczesny saved well from substitute Forssell. But this was Henry's night and at the final whistle he raised his arms to the heavens.

After the game he emerged from the dressing room to speak to the media:

I hope someone isn't going to wake me up and tell me it was a dream. I didn't know where to go, what to do. It was one of the best moments because it is the first time that I wore the Arsenal shirt being a fan. I became a fan when I left the club so now I know exactly how it feels to score for the club that you support. As I said earlier on to some of the guys in the dressing room, two weeks ago I was on holiday in Mexico on the beach and here I am scoring the winner against Leeds.

I never thought I was going to be here, talking to you after a game, so scoring a winner for the club that I love, I am actually dreaming right now.

Sunderland 1 Arsenal 2
Premier League
11 February 2012

Following Henry's match-winning goal against Leeds on his second Arsenal debut, the excitement of his return had somewhat fizzled out and he had failed to make an impact in any of his four ensuing cameo appearances from the bench. Furthermore, Arsenal's stuttering league form meant they faced a huge fight to retain their top-four position, with Tottenham looking increasingly likely to usurp them.

A 7-1 home victory against Blackburn, in which a late Henry strike was eventually given as an own goal by the Football Association's Dubious Goals Committee, had raised spirits, but if they were to retain their Champions League status Arsenal would now need to achieve the kind of consistency that had eluded them all season.

Hopes of silverware did remain alive thanks to their continued involvement in the FA Cup and Champions League, but an impending tie against Italian club AC Milan in the latter tournament looked a daunting task given Arsenal's patchy form. In any case, while Henry would still be around for the first leg in Italy, he was due to return to New York the following day, meaning he would miss the second leg at the Emirates.

It meant that Arsenal's match at Sunderland would be his penultimate appearance, and his last in the league. After resigning for the club, he modestly insisted that he had only come to lend a helping hand should the club need him. But at times that season, Arsenal had looked like only divine intervention would save them. Then again, many had hailed Henry's return to Arsenal as the Second Coming, so perhaps he was just the man to resurrect their hopes of finishing in the top four.

Team: Szczesny, Sagna, Mertesacker (72), Koscielny, Vermaelen, Oxlade-Chamberlain (66), Arteta, Song, Rosicky, Walcott (87), Van Persie
Subs: Henry (66), Ramsey (72), Arshavin (87)

Just as he had for all of his other appearances during his loan spell from New York Red Bulls, Henry started on the bench in what would be his last league appearance.

Sunderland's early efforts appeared to focus on disrupting Arsenal's rhythm and then hitting them on the break. The tactic was working well, with the pace of McClean and Sessegnon causing Arsenal problems and the home side could have had a penalty when the ball bounced off of Mertesacker's hand.

The second half began with neither side looking likely to break the deadlock and with 66 minutes gone Arsenal introduced Henry to proceedings, replacing Oxlade-Chamberlain.

But just 4 minutes later, Sunderland capitalised on an injury to Mertesacker by taking the lead. As the big German defender backtracked chasing a pass over the top, he went down clutching his ankle, leaving McClean to collect the ball and charge unimpeded towards Arsenal's goal. Entering the left-hand side of the penalty box, he unleashed a vicious shot across Szczesney and into the far corner of the net.

Mertesacker had to be carried off, but within 5 minutes Arsenal were level after the man who replaced him, Ramsey, hit a pea-roller from the edge of the box that hit the post and ricocheted onto the opposite post before trickling over the line.

Having forced themselves back into the game, Arsenal were desperate to claim all three points but they would have to wait until the death to do so. With 90 minutes on the clock, Arshavin launched a pin-point cross from the left and Henry ghosted between the Sunderland defence to direct a side-footed volley past Mignolet.

Henry ran to the Arsenal fans to celebrate his 228th goal for the club and one of the most important of them all. After the game he went back over and lapped up the adulation like the returning hero he had now become. After his protestations that he had only come to the club to 'lend a hand', the extent of his impact had blown such platitudes firmly out of the window. Arsenal quite simply could not afford to drop out of the Champions League, and Henry's last-gasp goal had gone some way to ensuring they would not suffer such a fate.

'I stayed a bit longer with the Arsenal fans because I knew it was my last game in the Premier League so I wanted to say "Thanks, that's it",' Henry said after the game. 'I felt like the kid who just came on and scored his first goal for the club he loves but, when it comes to Arsenal, I always feel something special.'

In his post-match interview, Arsène Wenger spoke about Henry's overall influence since returning.

He is more impressive than before because he only plays 20 minutes and he scores! We are grateful for what he has done for us in the short spell he had with us not only on the pitch but off the pitch; he was exceptional as well in the dressing room. We tried [to keep him for longer] but he has to go back, he is captain of his team and the season starts in two weeks.

It's a shame a player of that quality is not in England or Europe anymore. But he does a lot for football in America. Thierry finished the story of the legend today. He showed that exceptional talent survives.

But was it categorically the finish of the Henry story at Arsenal? When the man himself was asked, he remained playfully enigmatic. 'You can never say never. You have to ask the boss. When it comes to Arsenal it is difficult to say no. One day if they need any help I will be around.'

Postscript

As I write this in August 2014, with Thierry Henry into the fifth season of his New York odyssey and the twentieth of his professional career, rumours have begun to surface that he may soon retire from football.

Despite approaching his thirty-seventh birthday, the temptation to keep going must be strong for a player who in recent years has shown himself capable of still performing to a high level. Indeed, since his loan spell at Arsenal in 2012, there has not been a single MLS close-season in which he hasn't been linked with yet another return to the club that remains closest to Henry's heart.

'I've got a year left on my contract and I still feel good,' he said back in February this year. 'So I'm going to enjoy it and we'll see come the end of the year. You know yourself when it's the moment to go. When I get that feeling, I'll stop, but that's not yet the case.'

'But when I do retire, I think I will stay connected to football in some way. I feel good in New York, but my life is in London. I have my daughter there, my house. I think my future is in that city.'

With such deep roots already laid, it seems likely that London will at some point become his home once more. Ever the expressive, moody Frenchman on the pitch, not to mention a fine proponent of the Gallic shrug, off it he is an emblem of assimilation. Listen to him and you soon notice the cutesy English phraseology that has crept into his speech.

Whether in London or elsewhere, what will become of him after he departs his green dominion for the final time? Could he make the rare transition from great player to great manager? Certainly, he is a dedicated enough student of the game, as television viewers during his role as a pundit for the BBC at the recent 2014 World Cup in Brazil will testify. Perhaps the great unknown is whether Henry has the right temperament for the job, because what is clear is that most people do not believe they truly have the measure of the man.

It is for this reason that we are best to judge Henry as a footballer only – and for this the metrics are simple to measure. If the preceding pages have left any doubt, a glance ahead will reveal the remarkable sum total of his career achievements spanning two decades, his contribution to the football firmament laid bare for all to see.

A Career in Numbers

1 World Cup
1 European Championship
1 Confederations Cup
1 French Ligue 1
2 English Premier League
3 English FA Cup
1 UEFA Champions League
2 Spanish La Liga
1 Spanish Copa del Rey
1 Spanish Supercup
1 Major League Soccer Supporter's Shield
2 FIFA World Player of the Year runner-up
1 Ballon d'Or runner-up
3 English Football Writers' Association Footballer of the Year
2 English Professional Footballers' Association Player of the Year
4 French Player Of The Year
1 French Young Footballer of the Year
4 Premier League Golden Boot
2 European Golden Boot

Arsenal all-time leading goalscorer (228)
France all-time leading goalscorer (51)

Sources & Acknowledgements

The following publications have been quoted, referred to or used for research:

Books:
Auclair, Philippe, *Thierry Henry: Lonely at the Top* (2013).

Newspapers:
The Guardian
The Observer
Daily Telegraph
The Independent
The Sun
Daily Mirror
The New York Times

Magazines:
FourFourTwo
France Football

Websites:
www.arsenal.com
www.arseweb.com
www.espn.com
www.fifa.com
www.uefa.com
www.bbc.co.uk
www.goal.com